Charlotte Mary Yonge

Young Folks' History of Germany

Charlotte Mary Yonge

Young Folks' History of Germany

ISBN/EAN: 9783744781459

Printed in Europe, USA, Canada, Australia, Japan

Cover: Foto ©ninafisch / pixelio.de

More available books at **www.hansebooks.com**

OF

GERMANY.

BY
CHARLOTTE M. YONGE,

AUTHOR OF "THE HEIR OF REDCLYFFE," "BOOK OF
GOLDEN DEEDS," "YOUNG FOLKS' HISTORY OF
GREECE, &C.

CINCINNATI:
CRANSTON AND STOWE.
NEW YORK
HUNT AND EATON.

PREFACE.

THERE is here an endeavor to sketch the main outlines of the history of the German Empire, though the number of states, each with a separate history, makes it difficult to trace the line clearly. The names are, for the most part, given in their German form, rather than by their English equivalents.

CHARLOTTE M. YONGE.

ELDERFIELD, OTTERBOURN.

CONTENTS.

Chapter.	Page.
1.—The Ancient Germans	13
2.—Valhall	21
3.—The Germans and Romans. B.C. 60—A.D. 400	30
4.—The Nibelonig Heroes	40
5.—The Franks. 496—765	47
6.—Karl the Great. 768—814	60
7.—Ludwig I., the Pious. 814—840 Lothair I. 840—855. Ludwig II. 855—875. Karl II., the Bald. 875—876 Karloman. 876—880 Karl III., the Thick. 880—887 Arnulf. 887—899 Ludwig IV., the Child. 899—912	73
8.—Konrad I. 912—917 Heinrich I. 917—936 Otto I., the Great. 936—973	83
9.—The Saxon Emperors — Otto II., the Red. 973—983 Otto III., the Wonder. 983—1000 St. Heinrich II. 1000—1024	93

CONTENTS.

10.—The Franconian Line—
  Konrad II., the Salic. 1024—1039
  Heinrich III. 1039—1054
  Heinrich IV. 1054—1106
  Heinrich V. 1106—1114 } 104

11.—Lothar II. 1125—1137
  Konrad III. 1137—1152 } 116

12.—Friedrich I., Barbarossa. 1157—1178 . 127
13.—Friedrich I., Barbarossa (*continued*). 1174—1189
  Heinrich VI. 1189—1197 } 140

14.—Philip. 1198—1208
  Otto IV. 1209—1218 } 152

15.—Friedrich II. 1218 . 163
16.—Friedrich II. (*continued*). 1250 . 173
17.—Konrad IV. 1250—1254
  Wilhelm. 1254—1256
  Richard. 1256—1257 } 183

18.—Rodolf. 1278. . 192
19.—Adolf. 1291—1298
  Albrecht. 1298 } 201

20.—Heinrich VII. 1308—1313
  Ludwig V. 1313—1347 } 208

21.—Gunther. 1347—1347
  Karl IV. 1347—1378 } 217

22.—Wenzel. 1378—1400 . 224
23.—Ruprecht. 1400—1410.
  Jobst. 1410—1410
  Siegmund. 1411. } 233

24.—Albrecht II. 1438—1440
  Friedrich III. 1440—1482 } 243

25.—Friedrich III. 1482—1493 . 251
26.—Maximilian. 1493—1519 . 260
27.—Charles V. 1519—1529 . 270
28.—Charles V. 1530—1535 . 280
29.—Charles V. 1535 . 289
30.—Ferdinand I. 1556—1564 . 300
31.—Maximilian II. 1564 . 306
32.—Rudolf II. 1576—1612 . 313
33.—Matthias. 1612—1619 . 321
34.—The Revolt in Bohemia—
  Ferdinand II. 1619—1621 . 329

CONTENTS. vii.

35.—Gustaf Adolf and Wallenstein —
    Ferdinand II. 1621—1634 337
36.—Ferdinand II. 1634—1637
    Ferdinand III. 1637   .   .   . 349
37.—The Siege of Vienna —
    Leopold I. 1657—1687 .   .   . 358
38.—War of the Succession —
    Leopold I. 1685—1705 .   . 366
39.—Joseph I. 1705—1711   .   . 377
40.—Karl VI. 1711—1740   .   . 384
41.—Karl VII. 1740   .   .   . 392
42.—Franz I. 1745—1765 .   .   . 401
43.—Joseph II. 1765—1790 .   . 412
44.—Leopold II. 1790—1792 .   . . 423
45.—Franz II. 1792   .   .   . 429
46.—Franz II. 1804—1806   .   . . 435
47.—French Conquests —
    Interregnum. 1807—1815 .   . . 443
48.—Interregnum. 1815—1835 . •   . 456
49.—Interregnum. 1848   .   •   . 462
50.—Wilhelm I. 1870—1877   •   •   . 469

LIST OF ILLUSTRATIONS.

	PAGE.
Ancient German Village	15
Sacrifice to Woden	17
Volkyria	23
The Elves	27
The Velleda warning Drusus	31
Germanicus burying the Slain	33
Brunhild's Flight	49
Battle of Tours	53
St. Boniface felling the Oak	57
Karl the Great and Witikind	61
Karl the Great entering St. Peter's	65
Karl the Great in his School	67
Haroun al Raschid's Gifts	71
Ludwig the Pious	74
Odo appealing to Karl the Fat	81
The Last Tribute of the Magyars	85
Adelheid Hiding in the Corn	90
Otto's Flight	95
Opening the Tomb of Karl the Great	99
St. Henry	102
Heinrich IV. carried off	109
Penance of Heinrich IV.	113
Lothar II. leading the Pope's Horse	119
The Women of Weinsberg	123
Friedrich I. refuses the Milanese Submission	129
Faithfulness of Sieveneichen	133

List of Illustrations.

	PAGE
Friedrich I., kneeling to Heinrich the Lion	137
The Diet at Mainz	143
Richard the Lion Heart and Heinrich VI.	147
Heinrich VI.	150
Murder of Philip	155
Otto IV. finds his Bride dead	159
Friedrich II. putting on the Crown of Jerusalem	167
Friedrich II. receiving Isabel of England	175
Execution of Conradin and Friedrich	189
German Castle	193
Mediæval Costume	210
Heinrich VII.	213
Adolf	215
Karl IV.	222
Arnold von Winkelried	227
Wenzel	231
Huss at Constance	235
Siegmund	238
Albrecht II.	244
Friedrich III.	246
Maximilian and Albert Durer	255
Maximilian	261
Luther and his Thesis	265
Charles V.	271
Luther at Wartburg	275
Charles V. and Fugger	285
Flight of Charles V.	293
Charles V. in the Cloister, St. Just	297
Ferdinand I.	301
Maximilian II.	307
Rudolf and Tycho Brahe	315
Matthias	322
Friedrich V.	327

List of Illustrations.

	PAGE
Ferdinand II.	331
Wildenstein Castle	339
Gustaf Adolf	342
Death of Wallenstein	345
Bernhard of Saxe Weimar	350
Peace of Westphalia	355
Leopold I.	359
Friedrich I. King of Prussia (Coronation)	369
Marlborough and Eugene	373
Joseph I.	379
Karl VI.	385
Maria Theresa	393
Karl VII.	397
The Queen of Poland	405
Friedrich the Great and Zeithen	409
Maria Theresa and Kaunitz	415
Joseph II. holding the Plough	419
Leopold II.	427
Napoleon and Franz II.	437
Queen Louise pleading with Napoleon	445
Metternich and Napoleon	449
The Allies entering Paris	453
Wilhelm I.	473

YOUNG FOLKS' HISTORY OF GERMANY

CHAPTER I.

THE ANCIENT GERMANS.

THE history of the German Empire rightly begins with Karl the Great, but to understand it properly it will be better to go further back, when the Romans were beginning to know something about the wild tribes who lived to the north of Italy, and to the coast of the Gaulish or Keltic lands.

Almost all the nations in Europe seem to have come out of the north-west of Asia, one tribe after another, the fiercest driving the others farther and farther to the westward before them. Tribes of Kelts or Gauls had come first, but, though they were brave and fierce, they were not so sturdy as the great people that came after them, and were thus driven up into the lands bordering on the Atlantic Ocean; while the tribes that came behind them spread all over that middle part of Europe which lies between the Alps and the Baltic sea. These tribes all called themselves *Deutsch*, which meant the people; indeed, most of them do so still, though we English only call those Dutch who live in Holland. Sometimes they were called Ger, War, or Spear-men, just as the Romans were called Quirites; and this name, Spear-men or Germans, has come to be the usual name that is given to them together, instead of Deutsch as they call themselves, and from which the fine word Teutonic has been formed.

The country was full of marshes and forests, with ranges of hills in which large rivers rose and straggled, widening down to their swampy mouths. Bears and wolves, elks and buffaloes, ran wild, and were hunted by the men of the German tribes. These men lived in villages of rude huts, surrounded by lands to which all had a right in common, and where they grew their corn and fed their cattle. Their wives were much more respected than those of other nations; they were usually strong, brave women, able to advise their husbands and to aid them in the fight; and the authority of fathers and mothers over their families was great. The men were either freemen or nobles, and they had slaves, generally prisoners or the people of conquered countries. The villages were formed into what were called hundreds, over which, at a meeting of the freemen from all of them, a chief was elected from among the nobles; and many of the tribes had kings, who always belonged to one family, descended, it was thought, from their great god Woden.

ANCIENT GERMAN VILLAGE.

The German tribes all believed in the great god Woden, his brother Frey, and his son Thor, who reigned in a gorgeous palace, and with their children were called the Asa gods. Woden was all-wise, and two ravens whispered in his ear all that passed on the earth. The sun and moon were his eyes. The moon is so dull because he gave the sight of that eye for one draught of the well of wisdom at the foot of the great ash tree of life. He was a fearful god, who had stone altars on desolate heaths, where sacrifices of men and women were offered to him, and the fourth day of the week was sacred to him.

Frey was gentler, and friendship, faith, and freedom were all sacred to him. There is a little confusion as to whether Friday is called after him or Frigga, Odin's wife, to whom all fair things belonged, and who had priestesses among the German maidens. Thor, or, as some tribes called him, Thunder, was the bravest and most awful of the gods, and was armed with a hammer called Miölner, or the Miller or Crusher. Thunder was thought to be caused by his swinging it through the air, and the mark in honor of him was T, meant to be a likeness of his hammer. It was signed over boys when they were washed with water immediately after they were born; and in some tribes they were laid in their father's shields, and had their first food from the point of his sword.

These three were always the most honored of the Asa gods, though some tribes preferred one and

some the other; but Woden was always held to be the great father of all, and there were almost as many stories about the Asir as there were about the Greek gods, though we cannot be sure that all were known to all the tribes, and they were brought to their chief fulness in the branch of the race that dwelt in the far North, and who became Christians much later. Some beliefs, however, all had in common, and we may understand hints about the old faith of the other tribes by the more complete northern stories.

There was a great notion of battle going through everything. The Asa gods were summer gods, and their enemies were the forces of cold and darkness, the giants who lived in Jotenheim, the land of giants. All that was good was mixed up with light and summer in the old Deutsch notions; all that was bad with darkness and cold. Baldur, the son of Woden, was beautiful, good, and glorious; but Loki, the chief enemy, longed to kill him. His mother, Frigga, went round and made every creature and plant swear never to hurt Baldur, but she missed one plant, the mistletoe. So when all his brothers were amusing themselves by throwing things at Baldur, knowing they could not hurt him, Loki slyly put in the hand of his blind brother

Hodur a branch of mistletoe which struck him dead. But Frigga so wept and prayed that it was decreed that Baldur might live again provided everything would weep for him; and everything accordingly did weep, except one old hag who sat under a tree, and would shed no tears for Baldur, so he might not live, only he was given back to his mother for half the year, and then faded and vanished again for the other half. But Loki had his punishment, for he was chained under a crag with a serpent for ever dropping venom on his brow, though his wife was always catching it in a bowl, and it could only fall on him when she was gone to empty the bowl at the stream.

It is plain that Baldur meant the leaves and trees of summer, and that the weeping of everything was the melting of the ice; but there was mixed into the notion something much higher and greater respecting the struggle between good and evil.

CHAPTER II.

VALHALL.

THE hall of Woden was called Valhall,* and thither were thought to go the souls of the brave. There were believed to be maidens called Valkyr, or the choosers of the slain — Hilda, Guda, Truda, Mista, and others — who floated on swan's wings over the camps of armies before a battle and chose out who should be killed. Nor was such a death accounted a disaster, for to die bravely was the only way to the Hall of Woden, where the valiant enjoyed, on the other side of the rainbow bridge, the delights they cared for most in life — hunting the boar all day, and feasting on him all night; drinking mead from the skulls of their conquered enemies. Shooting stars were held to be the track of weapons carried to supply the fresh

Val meant a brave death in battle.

comers into Valhall. Only by dying gallantly could entrance be won there; and men would do anything rather than not die thus, rush on swords, leap from crags, drown themselves, and the like, for they believed that all who did not gain an entrance to the Hall of the Slain became the prisoners of Loki's pale daughter Hel, and had to live on in her cold, gloomy, sunless lands, sharing her bondage.

For once Loki and his children, and the other evil beings of the mist land, had made a fierce attack on Woden, and had all been beaten and bound. Fenris, the son of Loki, was a terrible wolf, who was made prisoner and was to be bound by a chain; but he would only stand still on condition that Tyr or Tiw, the son of Woden, should put his right hand into his mouth in token of good faith. The moment that Fenris found that he was chained, he closed his jaws and bit off the hand of Tiw, whose image therefore only had one hand, and who is the god after whom Tuesday is named.

Valhall was not, however, to last for ever. There was to come a terrible time called the Twilight of the Gods, when Loki and Fenris would burst their chains and attack the Asa gods; Woden would be slain by Fenris; Thor would perish in the flood of

Valkyria.

poison cast forth by the terrible serpent Midgard; and there would be a great outburst of fire, which would burn up Valhall and all within, as well as the powers of evil. Only two of the gods, Vidur and Wali, were to survive, and these would make again a new heaven and earth, in which the spirits of gods and men would lead a new and more glorious life.

How much of all this grew up later and was caught from Christianity we cannot tell; but there is reason to think that much of it was believed, and that heartily, making the German nations brave and true, and helping them to despise death. There were temples to the gods, where the three figures of Woden, Frey, and Thor were always together in rude carving, and sometimes with rough jewels for eyes. Woden also had sacred oaks, and the great stone altars on heaths, raised probably by an earlier race, were sacred to him. Sometimes human sacrifices were offered there, but more often sacred horses, for horses were the most sacred of their animals: they were kept in honor of the gods, auguries were drawn from their neighings, and at the great yearly feasts they were offered in sacrifice, and their flesh was eaten.

There were gods of the waters, Niord, and Egir,

who raised the great wave as the tide comes in at the mouth of rivers; and his cruel daughter Rana, who went about in a sea chariot causing shipwrecks. Witches called upon her when they wanted to raise storms and drown their enemies at sea.

One old German story held that Tiw* was the father of Man, and that man's three sons were Ing, Isk, and Er, the fathers of the chief Deutsch tribes. Isk (or Ash) was the father of the Franks and Allemans; Ing, of the Swedes, Angles, and Saxons; and Er, or Erman, of a tribe called by the Romans Herminiones. This same Er or Erman had a temple called Eresburg, with a marble pillar on which stood an armed warrior holding in one hand a banner bearing a rose, in the other a pair of scales; his crest was a cock; he had a bear on his breast, and on his shield was a lion in a field of flowers. A college of priests lived around; and before the army went out to battle, they galloped round and round the figure in full armor, brandishing their spears and praying for victory; and on their return they offered up in sacrifice, sometimes their prisoners, sometimes cowards who had fled from the foe.

The image was called Irmansul — *sul* meaning a pillar; and two pillars or posts were the great token

---

* The same word as the Greek Zeus and Latin Deus.

of home and settlement to the German nations. They were planted at the gate of their villages and towns, where one was called the Ermansaul, the other the Rolandsaul. And when a family were about to change their home, they uprooted the two wooden pillars of their own house and took them away. If they went by sea, they threw their pillars

THE ELVES.

overboard, and fixed themselves wherever these posts were cast up.

Dutch fancy filled the woods, hills, and streams with spirits. There were Elves throughout the woods and plains, shadowy creatures who sported in the night and watched over human beings for good or harm. The Bergmen dwelt in the hills, keeping guard over the metals and jewels hidden there, and forging wonderful swords that always struck home, and were sometimes given to lucky mortals, though they generally served for the fights in Valhall; and the waters had Necks and other spirits dangerous to those who loitered by the water-side. A great many of our best old fairy tales were part of the ancient German mythology, and have come down to our own times as stories told by parents to their children.

There were German women who acted as priestesses to Frigga, or Hertha, the Earth, as she was often called. She had a great temple in Rugen, an isle in the Baltic; her image was brought out thence at certain times, in a chariot drawn by white heifers, to bless the people and be washed in the Baltic waters. Orion's belt was called her distaff, and the gossamer marked her path over the fields when she brought summer with her.

When one of the northern tribes was going to start to the south to find new homes, their wives prayed to Frigga to give them good speed. She bade them stand forth the next morning in the rising sun with their long hair let down over their chins. "Who are these long beards?" asked Woden. "Thou hast given them a name, so thou must give them the victory," said Frigga; and henceforth the tribes were called Longbeards, or Lombards.

Before a battle, the matrons used to cast lots to guess how the fortunes of the day would go, doing below what the Valkyr did above. Sometimes a more than commonly wise woman would arise among them, and she was called the Wala, or Velleda, and looked up to and obeyed by all.

CHAPTER III.

THE GERMANS AND ROMANS.

B.C. 60—A.D. 400.

JUST as it was with the Britons and **Gauls,** the first we know of the Germans was when the Romans began to fight with them. When Julius Cæsar was in Gaul, there was a great chief among the tribe called Schwaben — Suevi, as the Romans made it — called Ehrfurst,* or, as in Latin, Ariovistus, who had been invited into Gaul to settle the quarrels of two tribes of Gauls in the north. This he did by conquering them both; but they then begged help from Cæsar, and Ehrfurst was beaten by the Romans and driven back. Cæsar then crossed the Rhine by a bridge of boats and ravaged the country, staying there for eighteen days. He was so struck with the bravery of the

* Honor prince.

The Velleda Warning Drusus.

Germans that he persuaded their young men to serve in his legions, where they were very useful; but they also learned to fight in the Roman fashion.

Germany was let alone till the time of the Emperor Augustus, when his step-son Drusus tried to make it a province of Rome, and built fifty fortresses along the Rhine, besides cutting a canal between that river and the Yssel, and sailing along the coasts of the North sea. He three times entered Germany, and in the year B.C. 9, after beating the Marchmen, was just going to cross the Elbe, when one of the Velledas, a woman of great stature, stood before the army and said, "Thou greedy robber! whither wouldst thou go? The end of thy misdeeds and of thy life is at hand." The Romans turned back dismayed; and thirty days later Drusus was killed by a fall from his horse.

Drusus' brother Tiberius went on with the attempt, and gained some land, while other tribes were allies of Rome, and all seemed likely to be conquered, when Quinctilius Varus, a Roman who came out to take the command, began to deal so rudely and harshly with the Germans that a young chief named Herman, of Arminius, was roused. He had secret meetings at night in the woods with other chiefs, and they swore to be faithful to one

another in the name of their gods. When all was ready, information was given to Varus that a tribe in the north had revolted. He would not listen to Siegert or Segestes, the honest German who advised him to be cautious and to keep Herman as a hostage, and set out with three legions to put it down; but his German guides led him into the thickest of the great Teutoberg forest, and the further they went the worse this grew. Trunks of trees blocked up the road, darts were hurled from behind trees, and when at last an open space was gained after three days' struggling through the wood, a huge host of foes was drawn up there, and in the dreadful fight that followed almost every Roman was cut off, and Varus threw himself on his own sword.

Herman married the daughter of Siegert, and was chief on the Hartz mountains, aided by his uncle Ingomar; but after five years, A.D. 14, the Emperor Tiberius sent the son of Drusus — who was called already, from his father's successes, Germanicus — against him. Some of the Germans, viewing Siegert as a friend of Rome, beset his village, and were going to burn it, when Germanicus came in time to disperse them and save Siegert. Thusnelda, the wife of Herman, was with her father, and was sent off as a prisoner to Rome with her baby; while Germanicus marched into the Teutoberg wood, found the bones of the army of Varus, and burnt them on a funeral pile, making a speech calling on his men to avenge their death. But Herman's horsemen fell on him and defeated him, and if the Germans had not been so eager to plunder they would have made a great many prisoners. They drove the Romans back across the Rhine, and the next year were ready for them, and had a tremendous battle on the banks of the Weser. In this the Romans prevailed, and Herman himself was badly wounded, and was only saved by the fleetness of his horse. However, he was not daunted, and still kept in the woods and harassed the Romans, once forcing them to take refuge in their ships.

Tiberius grew jealous of the love the army bore to Germanicus, and sent for him to return to Rome. Herman thus had saved his country, but he had come to expect more power than his chiefs thought his due, and he was slain by his own kinsmen, A.D. 19, when only thirty-seven years old. His wife and child had been shown in Germanicus' triumph, and he never seems to have seen them again. It was during this war that the great Roman historian

Tacitus came to learn the habits and manners of the Germans, and was so struck with their simple truth and bravery that he wrote an account of them, which seems meant as an example for the fallen and corrupt Romans of his time.

There were no more attempts to conquer Germany after this; but the Germans, in the year 69, helped in the rising of a Gaulish chief named Civilis against the Romans, and a Velleda who lived in a lonely tower in the forests near the Lippe encouraged him. He prevailed for a time, but then fell.

The Germans remained terrible to the Romans for many years, and there were fights all along the line of the empire, which their tribes often broke through; but nothing very remarkable happened till the sixth century, when there was a movement and change of place among them. This seems to have been caused by the Huns, a savage tribe of the great Slavonic or Tartar stock of nations, who came from the East, and drove the Deutsch nation, brave as they were, before them for a time.

Then it was that the Goths came over the Danube, and, dividing into the Eastern and Western Goths, sacked Rome, conquered the province of Africa, and founded two kingdoms in Spain and in

Northern Italy. Their great king Theuderick, who reigned at Verona, was called by the Germans Dietrich of Berne, and is greatly praised and honored in their old songs.

Then Vandals followed the Goths, and took Africa from them; and the Lombards, or Longbeards, after the death of Theuderick, took the lands in Northern Italy which had been held by the Goths, founded a kingdom, and called it Lombardy. The Burgundians (or Burg Castle men) gained the south-east part of Gaul all round the banks of the Rhone, and founded a kingdom there; and the Sachsen (sæx or axe men) settled themselves on the banks of the Elbe, whence went out bands of men who conquered the south of Britain. The Franks (free men) were, in the meantime, coming over the Rhine, and first plundering the north of Gaul, then settling there. All the western half of the Roman Empire was overspread by these Deutsch nations from the shores of the Baltic to the Mediterranean, from the Atlantic Ocean to the Carpathian Mountains; and instead of being conquered by the Romans, the Deutsch nations had conquered them.

It is chiefly with the Franks, Sachsen, Schwaben,

and Germans that this history is concerned; but before going any further, there is a great mythological story to be told, which all believed in as truth.

CHAPTER IV.

THE NIBELONG HEROES.

THERE are two versions of this strange ancient story — a northern one made in heathen times, a German one in Christian days. According to this one, the three gods, Woden, Loki, and Hamer, came down to a river in Nibelheim — the land of mist — to fish; and Loki killed an otter and skinned it. Now this otter was really a dwarf named Ottur, whose home was on the river bank, with his father and brothers, Fafner and Reginn, and who used to take the form of the beast when he wanted to catch fish. When his brothers saw what had befallen him, they demanded that Loki should, as the price of his blood, fill the otter's skin with gold; and this Loki did, but when he gave it, he laid it under a curse, that it should do no good to its owner.

The curse soon began to be fulfilled, for Fafner

killed his father to gain the treasure, and then
turned himself into a serpent to keep watch over
it, and prevent Reginn from getting it. But
Reginn had a pupil who was so strong that he
used to catch wild lions and hang them by the tail
over the wall of his castle. The northern people
called him Sigurd, but the Germans call him Siegfried,* and say that his father was the king of the
Netherlands, and that he was a hero in the train of
Dietrich of Berne. Reginn persuaded Siegfried to
attack the dragon Fafner and kill him, after which
he bade the champion bathe in the blood and eat
the heart. The bath made his skin so hard that
nothing could hurt him, except in one spot between
his shoulders, where a leaf had stuck as it was
blown down from the trees; and the heart made him
able to understand the voices of the birds. From
their song Siegfried found out that Reginn meant
to slay him, and he therefore killed Reginn and
himself took the treasure, in which he found a tarn
cap, which made him invisible when he put it on.
Serpents were called worms in old Deutsch, and
the Germans said that their city of Wurms was
the place where Siegfried killed the dragon. They
called him Siegfried the Horny.

* Conquering Peace.

Now there was a lady of matchless strength named Brunhild;* but she had offended Woden, who touched her with his sleep-thorn, so that she fell into a charmed sleep, surrounded with a hedge of flame. Siegfried heard of her, broke through the circle of fire, and woke the lady, winning her heart and love; but he had then to leave her in her castle after three days and go back to the common world, carrying her ring and girdle with him. But by a magic drink, as one story says, he was thrown into a sleep in which he lost all remembrance of Brunhild.

The great song of Germany, the *Nibelungen lied*, begins when Chriemhild,† the fair daughter of the king of Burgundy, had a dream in which she saw her favorite falcon torn to pieces by two eagles. Her mother told her that this meant her future husband, upon which she vowed that she would never marry. Soon after, Siegfried arrived and fell in love with her; but she feared to accept him because of her dream. However, the fame of Brunhild's beauty had reached the court, and Chriemhild's brother Gunther wanted to wed her. She would, however, marry no one who could not overcome her in racing and leaping; and as she was really

* Valkyr of the Breastplate. † Valkyr of the Hamlet.

one of the Valkyr, Gunther would have had no chance if Siegfried, still forgetful of all concerning Brunhild, had not put on his cap, made himself invisible, took the leap, holding Gunther in his arms, and drew him on in the race so as to give him the victory.

Then Gunther married Brunhild, and Siegfried Chriemhild. The first pair reigned in Burgundy, the second at Wurms, and all went well for ten years, when unhappily there was a great quarrel between the two ladies. The northern song says it was about which had the right to swim furthest out into the Rhine; the German, that it was which should go first into the Cathedral. Brunhild said that Siegfried was only Gunther's vassal; on which Chriemhild returned that it was to Siegfried, and not to her husband, that Brunhild had yielded, and in proof showed her the ring and girdle that he had stolen from her.

Brunhild was furiously enraged, and was determined to be revenged. She took council with Haghen, her husband's uncle, a wise and far-traveled man, whom every one thought so prudent that he was the very person whom poor Chriemhild consulted on her side as to the way of saving her husband. He had never loved Siegfried, and when his niece told him there was only one spot where her husband could be wounded, he bade her sew a patch on his garment just where it was, that he might be sure to know where to guard him. There was a great hunting match soon after, and Haghen contrived that all the wine should be left behind, so that all the hunters growing thirsty, lay down to drink at the stream, and thus Siegfried left defenceless the spot marked by his wife. There he was instantly stabbed by Haghen's contrivance. According to the heathen northern story, Brunhild, viewing herself as his true wife, burnt herself on a pile with his corpse in the Nibelung. She had only repented too late.

Chriemhild knew Haghen was the murderer, because the body bled at his touch; but she could not hinder him from taking away the treasure and hiding it in a cave beneath the waters of the Rhine. She laid up a vow of vengeance against him, but she could do nothing till she was wooed and won by Etzel or Atli, king of the Huns, on condition that he would avenge her on all her enemies. For thirteen years she bided her time, and then she caused her husband to invite Gunther and all the other Burgundians to a great feast at Etzelburg in Hungary. There she stirred up a terrible fight, of which the *Nibelungen lied* describes almost every blow. Dietrich of Berne at once rushed in and took King Etzel and Queen Chriemhild to a place of safety, keeping all his own men back while the fight went on — Folker, the mighty fiddler of Burgundy, fiddling wildly till he too joined in the fray, and then Dietrich's men burst in, and were all killed but old Sir Hildebrand, who, on his side, slew the mighty fiddler, so that of all the Burgundians only Gunther and Haghen were left. Dietrich then armed himself, made them both prisoners, and gave them up to Chriemhild; but in her deadly vengeance she killed them both; whereupon Hildebrand slew her as an act of justice, and, with Etzel and Dietrich, buried the dead.

I have told you this story in this place because two real personages, Attila the Hun and Theuderick of Verona, come into it, though there is no doubt that the story was much older than their time, and that they were worked into it when it was sung later. It shows what a terrible duty all the Deutsch thought vengeance was. There are stories in the north going on with the history of Siegfried's children, and others in Germany about Dietrich. It seems he had once had to do with Chriemhild in her youth, for she had a garden of roses seven miles round, guarded by twelve champions, and the hero who could conquer them was to receive from her a chaplet of roses and a kiss. Dietrich, Hildebrand, and ten more knights beat her champions, and took the crowns of roses, but would not have the kisses, because they thought Chriemhild a faithless lady!

In real truth, Attila, king of the Huns, lived fully one hundred years before the great Theuderick of Verona.

CHAPTER V.

THE FRANKS.

796–765.

THE most famous of the German tribes were the Franks, who lived on the banks of the Rhine, and were in two divisions, the Salian, so called because they once came from the river Yssel, and Ripuarians, so called from *ripa*, the Latin word for the bank of a river.

The Franks were terrible enemies to the Romans in the north-east corner of Gaul, and under their King Chlodio won a great many of the fifty fortresses that Drusus had built, in especial Trier and Köln, as they shortened the old name of Colonia, a colony. Chlodio only joined with the Romans to fight against that dreadful enemy of them all, Attila the Hun, who was beaten in the battle of Soissons. After his death, those of his people who did not go back to Asia remained on the banks of the Danube, and their country is still called Hungary.

The kings of these Franks were called Meerwings, from one of their forefathers. The only great man who rose up among them was Chlodwig,* who pushed on into Gaul, made Soissons his home, took Paris from the Gauls, and married Clotilda (famous Valkyr), the daughter of the Burgundian king, who was a Christian. The other Deutsch tribes went to war with Chlodwig, the Allemans especially; and it was in the midst of a battle with them, fought at Zulpich, that Chlodwig vowed that if Clotilda's God would give him the victory, he would worship Him rather than Freya or Woden. He did gain the victory, and was baptized by St. Remigius at Rheims, on Christmas Day, 496, with three thousand of his warriors. Most likely he thought that, as Gaul was a Christian country, he could only rule there by accepting the Christian's God; but he and his sons remained very fierce and wild. He conquered the Ripuarian Franks and made them one with his own people,

---

* The French call him Clovis, but he shall have his proper name here — Chlodwig, famous war.

and he also conquered the Goths in the South of France.

But when he died the kingdom was broken up among his sons, and they quarreled and fought, so that the whole story of these early Franks is full of shocking deeds. There were generally two kingdoms, called Oster-rik, eastern kingdom, and Ne-oster-rik, not eastern, or western kingdom, besides Burgundy, more to the south. The Oster-rik stretched out from the great rivers to the forests of the Allemans and Saxons, and was sometimes joined to the Ne-oster-rik. The chief freemen used to meet and settle their affairs in the month of March, and this was called a Marchfield; but the king had great power, and used it very badly.

It was never so badly used as by the widows of two of the long-haired kings, Hilperik and Siegbert, brothers who reigned in the West and East kingdoms. Siegbert's wife, Brunhild, was the daughter of the king of the Goths in Spain; Fredegond, the wife of Hilperik, was only a slave girl, and hated Brunhild so much that she had Siegbert murdered. The murders Fredegond was guilty of were beyond all measure. Her step-sons were killed by her messengers, and all who offended her were poisoned. When her husband died, she

reigned in the name of her son and then of her
grandson at Soissons, as Brunhild did at Metz.
Brunhild really tried to do good to her country,
and made some fine buildings, both churches and
convents; but she was fierce and proud, and drove
away the Irish priest Columbanus, when he tried
to rebuke her grandson Theuderick for his crimes.
Theuderick died in 613, leaving four sons; and
then Chlotar, Fredegond's grandson, attacked the
Oster-rik. Brunhild was old, and was hated by
her people; no one would fight for her, and she
tried in vain to escape. One of her grandsons
rode off on horseback and was never heard of more,
and the other three were seized with her. Fredegond was dead, but she had brought up Chlotar in
bitter hatred of Brunhild, and he accused her of
having caused the death of ten kings. He paraded
her through his camp on a camel, put her great-grand-
children to death before her eyes, and then had
her tied by the body to a tree and by the feet to a
wild horse, so that she died a horrible death.

After this the two kingdoms were joined together; but this wicked race of kings become so
dull and stupid that they could not manage their
own affairs, and they had, besides, granted away a
great many of their lands in fee, as it was called,

to their men, who were bound in return to do them service in war. These lands were called fiefs, and the holders of them were called Heer Zog — that is, army leaders — Duces (Dukes) in Latin; and Grafen, which properly meant judges, and whose Latin title was Comites (comrades), commonly called Counts. A city would have a Graf or Count to rule it for the king and manage its affairs at his court; and besides these who were really officers of the king, there were the Freiherren, or free lords, who held no office, and were bound only to come out when the nation was called on. They came to be also termed Barons, a word meaning man.

The kings lived on great farms near the cities in a rough sort of plenty, and went about in rude wagons drawn by oxen. The long-haired kings soon grew too lazy to lead the people out to war, and left everything to the chief of their officers, who was called the Mayor of the Palace.

Pippin* of Landen was a very famous Mayor of the Palace in the kingdom of the East Franks or Oster-rik, and his family had the same power after him. His grandson, Pippin of Herstall, Duke of the Franks, beat the West Franks at Testri in 687,

---

* A pet name for father.

and ruled over both kingdoms at once, though each had its own Meerwing king.

His son was Karl* of the Hammer, or Charles Martel, who was also Mayor of the Palace and Duke of the Franks, both East and West. He saved all Christendom from being overrun by the Saracen Arabs, by beating them in the great battle of Tours in 731.

His son was Pippin the Short, who had the same power at first, and became a great friend and helper to the Pope, who was much distressed by the Lombard kings in Northern Italy, who threatened to take Rome from him. Pope Zacharias rewarded Pippin by consenting to his becoming king of the Franks when the last of the Meerwings gave up his crown and went into a monastery.

Pippin's own subjects, the Franks, were Christians; but the tribes in Germany and Friesland still worshiped Woden and Thor. The English Church sent missionaries to them, and Pippin helped them as much as he could. The greatest was St. Boniface, who converted so many Germans that he was made Archbishop of Mainz, and this has always been the chief see in Germany. At Giesmar, the Hessians honored a great oak sacred to Thor, and

* A strong man.

St. Boniface Felling the Oak

Boniface found that even the Christians still feared the tree. He told them that if Thor was a god he would defend his own; then, at the head of all his clergy, he cut down the tree, and the people saw that Thor was no god. When he baptized them he made them renounce not only the devil, but Woden and all false gods. At last he was martyred by the heathen Frisians in 755.

CHAPTER VI.

KARL THE GREAT.

768–814.

BECAUSE of the help Pippin gave the Pope he was made a patrician of Rome; and, when he died in 768, his son Karl inherited the same rank. Karl was one of the mightiest and wisest of kings, who well deserves to be called the Great, for though he was warlike, he fought as much for his people's good as for his own power, and tried to make all around him wise and good. Wherever he heard of a good scholar, in Italy or in England, or in any part of Gaul, he sent for him to his court, and thus had a kind of school in his palace, where he and his sons tried to set the rough, fierce young Franks the example of learning from the Romans and their pupils the old Gauls. Karl could speak and read Latin as naturally as his own

Karl and Witikind.

native Deutsch; but he never could learn the art of writing, though he used to carry about tablets and practise when he had leisure. However, he had much really deep knowledge, and a great mind that knew how to make the best use of all kinds of learning.

All the German tribes were under him as king of the Franks except the Saxons, whose lands reached from the Elbe to Thuringia and the Rhine. They were heathens, who refused to listen to St. Boniface and his missionaries, and still honored the great idol at Eresbury called the Irmansaul. Karl invaded the land, overthrew this image, and hoped he had gained the submission of the Saxons, sending missionaries among them to teach them the truth; but they were still heathens at heart, and rose against him under their chief Witikind, so that the war altogether lasted thirty years. The Saxons rose against him again and again, and once so enraged him that he caused four thousand five hundred who had been made prisoners to be put to death; but still Witikind fought on till his strength was crushed. At last he submitted, and was brought to see Karl at Atigny, where they made friends, and Witikind consented to be baptized and to keep the peace.

When Witikind died, five years later, Karl made Saxony into eight bishoprics. He made bishops as powerful as he could, giving them guards of soldiers, and appointing them, when he could, Counts of the chief cities of their sees, because he could trust them better than the wild, rugged Frank nobles. The great bishoprics of Metz, Trier, and Köln rose to be princely states in this way.

While Karl was gone the first time to Saxony, the Lombard king, Desiderius, began to harass Rome again; and the Pope, Leo III., again sent to ask aid from Karl, who crossed the Alps, besieged Pavia, and sent the king into a monastery, while he was himself crowned with the iron crown that the Lombard kings had always worn. Then he went on to Rome, where he dismounted from his horse and walked in a grand procession to the Church of St. Peter on the Vatican hill, kissing each step of the staircase before he mounted it, in remembrance of the holy men who had trodden there before him. In the church the pope received him, while the choir chanted "Blessed be he that cometh in the Name of the Lord."

But the Lombards chose the son of their late king for their leader, and there was another war which ended in their being quite crushed. Karl also

Karl the Great Entering St. Peter's.

gained great victories over the Moors in Spain, and won the whole of the country as far as the Ebro; but the wild people of the Pyrenees, though they were Christians, were jealous of his power, and rose on his army as it was returning in the Pass of Roncesvalles, cutting off the hindmost of them especially Roland, the warden of the marches of Brittany, about whom there are almost as many stories as about the heroes of the Nibelung.

He had another great war with the Avars and Bohemians, people of Slavonic race, who lived to the eastward of the Deutsch, and had ringforts or castles consisting of rings of high walls, one within another. One of the Swabians who fought under Karl was said, at the taking of one of these forts, to have run his spear through seven of the enemy, at once! The ringforts were taken, and Karl appointed all around the border or marches of his kingdoms March-counts, Mark-grafen, or Marquesses, who were to guard the people within from the wild tribes without. One mark was Karnthen or Carinthia, going from the Adriatic to the Danube; another was Œsterreich or Austria, the East Mark; and another was Brandenburg. All the countries in his dominion were visited four times a year by officers who made reports to him, and

judged causes; but if people were not satisfied, they might appeal to the Palace judge, or Pfalzgraf—Palgraf, as he was called.

His lands streached from the Baltic Sea to the Mediterranean and the Ebro, from the Bay of Biscay to the borders of the Huns and Avars; and when he held his great court at Paderborn in 729 he had people there from all the countries round, and even the great Khalif Haroun al Raschid (the same of whom we hear so much in the *Arabian Nights*) being likewise an enemy of the Moors in Spain, sent gifts to the great king of the Franks — an elephant, a beautiful tent, a set of costly chessmen, and a water-clock, so arranged that at every hour a little brazen ball fell into a brass basin, and little figures of knights, from one to twelve, according to the hour, came out and paraded about in front.

Pope Leo X. came likewise to Paderborn, and by his invitation Karl made a third visit to Rome in the year 800, and was then made Emperor of the West. The old Roman Empire was revived in him, the citizens shouting, "Long live Carolus Augustus the Cæsar;" and from that time Cæsar, or, as the Germans call it, Kaisar, has always been the title of Karl's successors in what he called the Holy Roman Empire, as he held his power from the Church, and meant to use it for God's glory. The empire was a gathering of kingdoms — namely, the old Frank Oster-rik and Ne-oster-rik, Germany, the kingdom of Aquitane, the kingdom of Burgundy, of Lombardy, and Italy. Karl was king of each of these, but he meant to divide them between his sons and Bernhard,* king of Italy. The little Ludwig, at three years old, was dressed in royal robes and sent to take possession of Aquitaine, while Karl himself reigned at Aachen, where he built a grand palace and cathedral. His two elder sons died young, and when the Kaisar fell sick at Aachen, Ludwig was his only son. He took the youth into the cathedral, made him swear to fear and love God, defend the Church, love his people, and keep a conscience void of offence, and then bade him take the crown off the altar and put it on his own head. Karl lived a year after this, and died in 814, one of the greatest men who ever lived.

* Firm Bears.

Haroun Al Raschid's Gifts.

CHAPTER VII.

LUDWIG I., THE PIOUS, ... 814–840.
LOTHAR I., ... 840–855.
LUDWIG II., ... 855–875.
KARL II., THE BALD, ... 875–876.
KARLOMAN, ... 876–880.
KARL III., THE THICK, ... 880–887.
ARNULF, ... 887–899.
LUDWIG IV., THE CHILD, ... 899–912.

LUDWIG THE PIOUS is the same emperor as he whom the French call Louis the debonair, but it is better to use his real name, which is only a little softened from Chlodwig. He was a good, gentle man, but he had not such strength or skill as his father to rule that great empire, and he was much too easily led. He was crowned Emperor by Pope Stephen, and then gave kingdoms to his sons; Lothar * had the Rhineland, the old home of the Franks, and was joined in the empire with his father; Pippin had

* Famous Warrior.

Aquitaine, and Ludwig Bavaria; but none of them were to make peace or war without consent of the Emperor. Bernhard, King of Italy, their cousin, did not choose to reign on these terms, and marched against the Emperor, but was defeated, made prisoner, condemned by the Franks, and put

LUDWIG THE PIOUS.

to death. Lothar had his kingdom, and was suspected of having prevented him from being pardoned; but the Emperor always grieved over his death as a great sin.

In 814, Ludwig I. lost his wife, and soon after married a Bavarian lady named Judith, who had a son named Karl. Ludwig wanted a kingdom for this boy, and called a diet at Wurms, where a new kingdom called Germany was carved out for him; but this greatly offended his brothers, who rose against their father, and overcame him. They wanted to drive him into becoming a monk, but this he would not do, and his German subjects rose in his favour, and set him on his throne again.

He forgave his sons, and sent them back to their kingdoms; but in a few years they were all up in arms again, and met the Emperor near Colmar. All Ludwig's men deserted him when the battle was about to begin, so that the place was afterwards called the Field of Falsehood. The Emperor fell into his sons' hands, and Lothar, in the hope of keeping him from reigning again, persuaded the clergy to tell him it was his duty to submit to penance of the higher degree, after which nobody was allowed to command an army. The meek Emperor, who had always reproached himself for Bernhard's death, was willing to humble himself, and, stripped off his robes, he lay on a couch of sackcloth and read a list of his sins, which had been drawn up by his foes, and made him confess not only that he had been unjust to Bernhard, but that he had been a blasphemer, a perjured wretch, and fomenter of strife. Then thirty bishops, one after the other, laid their hands on his head, while the penitential psalms were sung, and all the time Lothar looked on from a throne rejoicing in his father's humiliation. But his pride had shocked every one, and his two brothers, with a number of Franks, rose and rescued the Emperor from him, treating their father with all love and honor, and the bishops bidding him resume his sword and belt. Even Lothar was obliged to come to him and say, "Father, I have sinned against heaven and in thy sight," and the gentle old man kissed him, and sent him to Italy.

When Pippin died there was a fresh war, for the people of Aquitaine would allow no Franks to come near his son, from whom therefore Ludwig took the kingdom, and there was much fighting and many horrors, all made worse by the ravages of the heathen Northmen and Danes. At Wurms, a treaty was made by which Lothar was to have all the eastern half of the empire, Karl all the western, leaving young Ludwig only Bavaria. Ludwig, in his anger, took up arms, and just as the war was beginning, the good gentle old Emperor became so ill that he retired to an island in the Rhine named Ingelheim, and there died. The priest who attended him asked if he forgave his son. * Freely do I forgive him," said the old man; "but fail not to warn him that he has brought down my grey hairs with sorrow to the grave." Ludwig I. died in 840, in his sixty-third year.

Karl then joined Ludwig against Lothar, and at Fontanet, near Auxerre, there was a desperate battle, 150,000 men on each side, with a front six miles long to each army. The fight lasted six hours, and Lothar was beaten; but his brothers seem to have been shocked at their own victory over a brother and an emperor, and there was a fast of three days after it. They soon after made peace at the treaty of Verdun, in 843, by which Ludwig had the countries between the Rhine, the North Sea, the Elbe, and the Alps — what in fact is now called Germany. Lothar had, besides Italy, all the Rhineland, and the country between the Scheldt, the Meuse, the Saone, and the Rhone. This was called Lothar's portion, or Lotharingia, and part is still called Lorraine.

Karl's portion was all to the west of this, and was then called Karolingia, after his name, but it did not keep the title, and after a time came to be known as France.

Ludwig II., King of Germany, was much tormented, both by the Northmen and the Slavonic nations to the east, Avars, Bohemians, or Czechs, as they call themselves, and the Magyars, who lived in the country once settled by Attila's Huns, and therefore called Hungary. There is a story that, when the Saxons and Thuringians came home defeated from a battle with these people, their wives rose up and flogged them well for their cowardice.

Lothar I., the Emperor, died in 855, and his son Ludwig is counted as the second Kaisar of the name, but he died without children, in 875, and then there was a war between all his brothers and Ludwig, King of Germany, and Karl, of Karolingia; ending in Karl, who was commonly called the Bald, becoming Kaisar Karl II.; but he had many more kingdoms on his hands than he could manage, and was terribly tormented with the Northmen, besides having quarrels on his hands with all his nephews. His brother Ludwig of Germany made matters worse by dividing his kingdom into three at his death, in 876, for his three sons. Karloman, the eldest of these, attacked the Kaisar, and drove him to the alps, where he died at the foot of Mount Cenis, in 877, after a miserable reign.

Karloman then became Emperor. He was also King of Bavaria and of Italy, and his next brother

Ludwig was King of Saxony, where an old chronicler says that his life was useless alike to himself, the Church, and his kingdom; and so, when Karloman died, the empire was given to the youngest brother, Karl III.,* called der Dicke, the Thick, who turned out not to be much wiser or more active. In his time the Northmen made worse inroads than ever; and though on the death of his cousin, called Louis the Stammerer, France likewise fell to him, he was quite unable to protect his people anywhere; and when the Count of Paris forced his way through the Northern fleet in the Seine, and came to beg his help, he could do nothing but offer a sum of money to buy them off, Everybody was weary of him, and at last an assembly was held at Tribur, on the Rhine, which declared him unfit to rule, and sent him into a monastery, where he died in two months, in 888. Arnulf, a son of Karloman, was made Emperor, but the French took the brave Count of Paris for their king, and France never formed part of the empire again. Arnulf was a brave Kaiser, and so beat off the Northmen that they never greatly molested Germany again; but he died young, in

---

* The French call him Charles le Gros and he is generally termed the Fat, but Thick seems to express dullness as well as stoutness.

890, when his son Ludwig III., called the Child, was only six years old. He had a stormy reign, so tormented by the Magyars, who were trying to push beyond Hungary, that he died of grief, quite worn out, in 912.

CHAPTER VIII.

KONRAD I., ... 912–917.
HEINRICH I., ... 917–936.
OTTO I. THE GREAT, ... 936–973.

AS the Karling line was worn out, the German nobles chose another Frank, Konrad,* Count of Franconia, for their king, and when at the end of six years he died, he bade them choose in his stead Count Heinrich † of Saxony, who had been his enemy, and beat him in a great battle, but whom he thought the only man who had skill enough to defend Germany.

Heinrich was hawking on the Harz Mountains when the news of this advice was brought to him, and he is therefore called Heinrich the Fowler. He was wise and brave, and brought all the great dukedoms of Germany under his rule. These were, besides Saxony, Franconia, Swabia, Bavaria, and Lorraine. His great wars were with the Magyars

* Bold Speech. † Home Ruler.

in Hungary. Though he beat them in one battle, he was forced to make a truce for nine years, and pay them tribute in gold all the time. During all that time he was preparing himself and his people, and training his nobles to fight on horseback, by games which some people say were the beginning of tournaments. The men of lower rank were to be also trained to fight from the time they were thirteen years old, and to meet near the villages every three days to practise the use of arms. Besides, he saw that the great want was of walled cities, where the people might take shelter from their enemies; so he built towns and walled them in, and commanded that one man out of every nine should live in a *bury*, as these fortresses were called. Thus began the burghers of Germany. The public meetings, fairs, markets, and feasts were to take place within the towns, and justice was to be dealt out there. Stores were to be kept in case of a siege, and the country people were to send in a part of their produce to supply them, and in this way they were made the great gathering-places of the country.

When Heinrich thought the country quite ready to fight against the Magyars, he defied them when next they sent for tribute, by giving them nothing

The Last Tribute of the Macgregors.

but a wretched mangy dog. The next year they entered Germany to punish him, but he beat them at Keuschberg. Then they lighted beacon fires on the hills to rouse their people, and a great multitude mustered to overwhelm the Germans; at this same place, Keuschberg, Heinrich unfolded the banner of St. Michael, and rushed on the enemy, all his men crying out the Greek response, "*Kyrie eleison*," "Lord, have mercy," while the Magyars answered with wild shouts of "Hui! Hui!" but they were totally defeated, and driven back within Hungary. After this his troops hailed him as Emperor. He also conquered the Duke of Bohemia, and made him do homage to the kingdom of Germany. He beat back the Wends, who lived on the marshes of the Baltic Sea east of the Saxons, and were their great enemies; and he also tried to drive back the Danes. He tried to get these nations to become Christians, but he only succeeded with some of the Bohemians, where the good Duke Wenceslaf was a Christian, already, thanks to his mother, St. Ludmilla. He is the same of whom the pretty story is told that we have in the ballad of "Good King Wenceslas," though he was not really a king. He was murdered by his wicked brother Boleslaf, and the Christians were persecuted for some years.

The good King Heinrich meant to go to Rome to be crowned Kaisar by the Pope, but he never could be spared long enough from home, and died in the year 936.

His son Otto had been already chosen King of Germany, and was married to Edith, sister to the English king Athelstan, a gentle lady, who saved and petted a deer which had taken refuge in her chamber. He was crowned at Aachen by the archbishop of Mainz, and the great dukes were present in right of their offices — the Duke of Franconia, as carver; the Duke of Lorraine, as chamberlain; the Duke of Swabia, as cup-bearer; the Duke of Bavaria, as master of the horse. Standing in the middle aisle of the cathedral, the archbishop called on all who would have Otto for their king to hold up their right hands. Then, leading him to the Altar, he gave him the sword to chastise the enemies of Christ, the mantle of peace, the sceptre of power, and then, anointing head, breast, arms, and hands with oil, crowned him with the golden crown of Karl the Great; and there was a great feast, when all the dukes served him according to their offices; but he had a stormy reign. The Dukes of Franconia, and Lorraine rebelled, and so did his own brothers; but he was both brave, wise, and forgiving, so he brought them all to submit, and forced Boleslaf of Bohemia to leave off persecuting the Christians.

The Karling King of France, Louis IV., had a great quarrel with his vassals, Hugh, Count of Paris, and Richard, Duke of Normandy, who called in the help of Harald Blue-tooth, King of Denmark. Louis had married another English princess, and Otto came to help his brother-in-law, thus beginning a war with Harald which ended in his making Denmark subject to the empire; and he also subdued the Slavonic Duchy of Poland. He founded bishoprics, like Karl the Great, wherever he conquered heathens, and sent missions with them. Magdeburg was one of his great bishoprics.

The Karling line of Kings of Italy had come to an end with King Lothar, who had been married to Adelheid, a Karling herself. She was young and beautiful, and the Lombard duke, Berenger of Ivrea, wanted to marry her to his son. When she refused, he shut her up in a castle on the Lago di Garda; but a good monk named Martin made a hole through the walls of her dungeon, and led her wandering about, traveling by night, and hiding by day in the standing corn and reeds, till she reached a fisherman's hut, where she remained for some days in the dress of a fisher-boy, while Brother Martin carried news to her friends. They took her to the castle of Canossa, and sent to entreat the help of Otto. He had lost his English wife; so Adelheid offered to marry him, and give him her

ADELHEID HIDING IN THE CORN.

claim to the kingdom of Italy. He collected his troops, and came down on Berenger, who was besieging Canossa, drove him away, and, taking the Queen in triumph to Pavia, held at once his wedding and his coronation as King of the Lombards.

He was, however, not at peace, for his son

Ludolf, **Duke of Swabia**, rebelled against him, out of jealousy of **his** brother Heinrich; but he was tamed at last, and came barefoot to kneel at his father's feet for pardon, which the King gave him, but he forfeited his dukedom, and was sent to Italy. After this he had another terrible war with the Magyars, ending in a most horrible battle on the Lech, when the river ran red with blood, and out of 60,000 Magyars only seven came home to tell the tale, and those with slit noses and ears. The Germans on the field of battle hailed Otto as Kaisar; and as he was soon after called into Italy to set to rights the disorder caused by Ludolf's bad management, he went to Rome, and was crowned Emperor, while his son Otto was crowned King of the Germans, at Aachen, in 961. Things were in a sad state at Rome. The Popes were now so powerful **that** ambitious men wanted to be Popes, and there was bribery, fighting, and murder to gain the holy office. So Otto called a council of Bishops, and tried to bring things into better order, but when he went away they soon fell back again, and great crimes were committed.

Otto had nearly as large an empire as Karl the Great, for if he had less to the west and south, he **had** more to the north and east. He was well named the great, for he was a good and pious, wise and warlike man. He spent his last years mostly in Italy, but he died, in 973, at Memleben, while kneeling before the altar in the church, so peacefully that he was thought to be only asleep. He was buried at Magdeburg, beside his first wife, the English Edith.

CHAPTER IX.

THE SAXON EMPERORS.

OTTO II., THE RED, ... 973- 983.
OTTO III., THE WONDER, ... 983-1000.
ST. HEINRICH II., ... 1000-1024.

OTTO II. was called the Red, and was but nineteen years old when his father died, though he had been already crowned and married. His wife was Theophano, daughter of the Eastern Emperor Nicephorus. Bishop Liutprand had been sent to ask her of her father, but was greatly displeased with Constantinople, where the Emperor told him that the Germans would only fight when they were drunk, and that their weapons were too heavy to use. Also, he said that there were no real Romans save at Constantinople, and made a sign with his hand to shut Liutprand's mouth when he began to speak. The Eastern Cæsars no doubt greatly despised the attempt of the barbarous Germans to call themselves Kaisars, while the German Bishop thought 400 stout Germans could have beaten their whole army, and called Constantinople a "perjured, lying, cheating, rapacious, greedy, avaricious, nasty town."

Otto was so young that almost all the great dukes whom his father had forced to do homage hoped to shake off his yoke, but he reduced them all. Then Lothar, King of France, went to war with him, and swore that he would drink up all the rivers in Germany; to which Otto replied that he would cover all France with straw hats, for the Saxon troops used to go out to war in summer with straw hats over their hemlets. Charles, the brother of Lothar, marched through Lorraine and seized Aachen, where he turned the golden eagle on the roof of the palace of Charles the great with his beak towards France; but Otto met him there, routed him, and hunted him back to Paris. There, while the Germans besieged the city, Lothar offered to settle the matter by a single combat with Otto, but the Germans answered, "We always heard that the Franks set little store by their King, and now we see it." They could not take the city, and concluded a peace, by which the right of the empire to Lorraine was established.

Otto's Flight.

Otto was the son of the Empress Adelheid, and thus was half Italian, and he cared very much for the affairs of Italy. Rome was in a dreadful state, for the people had hated having Popes thrust on them by German Emperors, and broke out again and again. One Pope had just been murdered, and another set up in his place, and Otto thought it was time to interfere with a high hand, and also a cruel one; so he came to Rome, and inviting the chief citizens to a feast in the open space before St. Peter's Church, there seized and put to death all whom he thought dangerous to the authority of Rome.

The southern provinces of Italy had been promised him as the portion of his wife Theophano, but as they were not given up to him, he marched to take possession of them; but the Greek Emperor had allied himself with a body of Saracens who had settled in part of Sicily, and Otto met with a terrible defeat at Basantello in Calabria. He had lost his horse in the battle, and made for the sea-shore on foot. A Jewish rabbi, coming by offered him his horse, and on this horse, with the shouts of the pursuing Saracens still ringing in his ears, the Emperor dashed into the sea towards a Greek ship, which took him on board. He spoke Greek so well that no one found out he was a German; and though one Slavonic merchant was there who knew him, he did not betray him, but contrived that the ship should put in at the city of Rossano, where Otto escaped unperceived, and swam ashore. There he found his wife Theophano, but she, as a Greek, was proud of the victory of her nation, and instead of comforting him, scornfully said, "How my countrymen have frightened you!" Otto took this bitterly to heart, and meant to assemble a fresh army and retrieve his cause, but his health had been hurt by his campaign, and he grew so ill that he called a Diet at Verona, and obtained of his nobles the assurance that they would choose his three-year-old son King of Germany and Kaisar, and that the two Empresses, Theophano and Adelheid, should govern in his name. He died in the year 983, when only twenty-nine years old.

Otto III. was carefully brought up by his mother, and Gerbert, Abbot of Magdeburg, and was so learned that he was called the Wonder of the World. He was brave and able, and was only sixteen when he went to Rome and was crowned Emperor. His design was to make Rome his capital, reign there as Western Emperor, and render Germany only a province; and he made his tutor, Gerbert, Pope.

Opening the Tomb of Karl the Great

But his schemes were cut short by his death in 1000, in the city of Paterno, having spent very little of his short life in Germany, though he chose to be buried at Aachen, where shortly before he had opened the tomb of Karl the Great, and found the robed, crowned, and sceptred corpse sitting undecayed on its chair of state just as it had been placed 200 years before.

This year, 1000, was that when the end of the world was expected daily to happen, and it had a great effect upon the whole world. Heinrich, Duke of Bavaria, Otto's cousin through a daughter of Otto the Great, was elected in his place, and was so devout that he and his wife Kunigund* of Luxemburg are both reckoned as saints. He endowed the Bishopric of Bamberg with lands of his own, and therefore is generally drawn with the model of the cathedral in his arms. He was crowned Emperor at Rome, and as he, like Otto, held that the Kings of the Germans had the right of reigning over Rome and Italy, he took the title of King of the Romans. Thenceforth the German Kings were so called until they were crowned as Emperors at Rome. An Emperor was usually crowned four times — at Aachen, as King of the Romans, which

* Bold War.

really meant of Germany; at Pavia, of Italy; at Monza, of Lombardy, with an iron crown, said to be made partly of one of the nails of the cross; and at Rome, as Kaisar or Emperor. It was the choice

ST. HENRY.

of the nobles of Germany which gave him all these rights, though he was never Kaisar till his coronation by the Emperor. St. Heinrich did all he could to promote the conversion of the Slavonic nations round him, and was a friend and helper of the good King Stephen of Hungary. The last event of his life was going to make a visit to Robert, King of France, a man as pious and saintly as himself. He died on his way back, in 1024, the last of the Saxon Emperors.

CHAPTER X.

THE FRANCONIAN LINE.

```
KONRAD II., THE SALIC, .. 1024–1039.
HEINRICH III., ............ 1039–1054.
HEINRICH IV., ............. 1054–1106.
HEINRICH V., .............. 1106–1114.
```

THE German dukes, archbishops, counts, bishops, and great abbots all met on a plain near Mainz, on the banks of the Rhine, to choose a new king. Two Konrads of Franconia, both cousins, and descended from a daughter of Otto the Great, stood foremost, and they agreed that whichever was elected should receive the ready submission of the other. The elder one, who was chosen, is known as Konrad the Salic, because he traced his descent from the old Meerwing kings; but neither he nor his family resembled them in indolence. With the help of his son Heinrich, he did much to pull down the power of the dukes, and he favored the great free cities, which were fast growing into strength.

Konrad was crowned Emperor in 1027, and had two kings present at the ceremony — Rudolf, the last King of Burgundy, and our own Danish King Knut, whose daughter Kunhild married Heinrich, the son of the Kaisar. The Kaisar's own wife was Gisela, niece of Rudolf, who on his death left the kingdom to him. This did not mean the duchy of Burgundy, which belonged to France, but the old kingdom of Arles, or Provence, Dauphine, Savoy, and part of Switzerland, over which the Kings of Germany continued to have rights.

Konrad had wars with the Bohemians and Hungarians, but gained the advantage with both, and he was also a great law-maker. In his time it was settled that lands should not be freshly granted on the death of the holder, but should always go on to the next heir; and that no man should forfeit his fief save by the judgment of his peers, thus preventing the dukes and counts from taking away the grants to their vassals at their own will. He died in 1039, and was buried at Speyer.

His son Heinrich III. was twenty-two when he began to reign, and was well able to carry out his father's policy, so far as spirit and resolution went.

The quarrels at Rome were worse than ever, there being no less than three Popes, and he marched to Rome, sent them all into monasteries, and set up one of his own choosing, namely, Clement II. Indeed, though his was but a short reign, he was the maker of no less than four Popes, for each died almost as soon as he was appointed; but there was a strong feeling growing up that this was not the right way for the head of the Western Church to be chosen, and it was most strongly felt by a young Roman deacon called Hildebrand, who resolved to make a reformation.

Things grew worse when Heinrich III. died in the flower of his age, in 1054, leaving a little son, Heinrich IV., of five years old, under the charge of his mother, Agnes, a good woman, but not strong enough to keep the great dukes in order; and she tried to bribe her enemies by giving them lands, which only made them more able to do her mischief. The Church lands, the great bishoprics and abbeys, were given either by favor, fear, or money, and some dioceses went from father to son, like duchies and counties, and the clergy were getting to be as bad as the laity. To check all this, Hildebrand led Pope Stephen II. to forbid all priests, even those who were not monks, to marry; and also a great council was collected at Rome, at the Lateran Gate, where it was decreed that henceforth no clergyman should ever receive any benefice from the hands of a layman, but the bishops should be chosen by their clergy, and the Pope himself by the seventy chief clergy of Rome, who were called cardinals, and wore scarlet robes and hats, in memory of the old Roman purple. This was in the year 1059.

Three years later the great nobles of Germany resolved to be rid of the rule of the Empress Agnes. Hanno, archbishop of Köln, invited her and her son to spend the Easter of 1062 at the island of Kaiserswerth, on the Rhine, and while there the young Heinrich was invited on board a pleasure-boat, which instantly pushed off for the mainland. The boy, then thirteen years old, tried to leap out and swim back to his mother, but he was held back; and though his mother stood weeping and begging for help, no one would do anything but yell at those who were rowing the boat rapidly to Köln, where Hanno proclaimed himself Regent, and declared that the affairs of the kingdom should be managed by the bishop of whatever diocese the King was in.

Hanno hoped thus to rule the kingdom, but his

plan turned against him, for Adalbert, Bishop of Bremen, got Heinrich into his power, and kept him amused with constant feasting and revelry, which did his whole character much mischief; and he learnt besides to dislike and distrust all the great dukes and nobles.

When he came of age he kept Adalbert as his chief adviser, and was very harsh and fierce to his subjects, especially the Saxons. There was a rising against him, and he was forced to send away Adalbert, and marry Beatha, the daughter of the Margrave of Susa; but he hated and ill-used her, and his court was a place of grievous wickedness, while there was constant war with his people.

In the meantime Hildebrand had been chosen Pope, in the year 1073, and he at once began to enforce the decrees of the Lateran Council, of which the Germans had taken no notice. The decree was read aloud at Efrurt by the Archbishop of Mainz to a synod of bishops, and such a roar of fury rose that his life was in danger, and Heinrich thought his subjects would all hold with him in resisting it.

But Heinrich's violence and harshness had set his people against him, and the Saxons appealed to Rome against his injustice. Gregory VII. sum-

moned him to Rome to answer their charges, excommunicating at the same time all the bishops who had obtained their sees improperly. Upon this Heinrich called together the German bishops at Wurms, and made them depose the Pope. Gregory replied by pronouncing the King deposed, and releasing his subjects from their oath of allegiance. Germany and Italy were divided between the Pope and the King, and the Germans agreed that unless the King were absolved within the year they must regard him as deposed, and choose another in his stead. Heinrich felt that he must give way, and he made a most dangerous winter journey across the Alps by Mont Cenis, with Bertha and her child, blinded by snow or sliding along in frost. The Queen and her child were wrapped in an ox-hide, and dragged along in a sledge.

In Lombardy the bishops and nobles were favorable to Heinrich, but he only sought to make his peace with the Pope, and hastened to Canossa, the castle of Countess Matilda of Tuscany, Gregory's greatest friend, where the Pope then was. He came barefooted and bareheaded, in the hair shirt of a penitent, and was kept for three days thus doing penance in the court of the castle before he was admitted to the chapel, where the Pope absolved him, but only on condition that, till the affairs of Germany should be settled by the Pope, he should not assume his place as King. Nor had his humiliation hindered the Germans, who hated him, from electing a new king, Rudolf of Swabia, who was called the Priests' King. All Germany was thus at war, and Heinrich declared that Swabia was forfeited, and gave it to Friedrich of Hohenstaufen, who had married his daughter Agnes. Gregory, after a time, took the part of Rudolf, and Heinrich, on his side, appointed a Pope of his own; so that there were two Popes and two Kings of the Romans, until the battle of Zeitz, where Rudolf's right hand was cut off by Gottfried of Bouillon, and he was afterwards killed.

After this Heinrich prevailed, and pushed into Italy, where he beat Matilda's army, and besieged Rome for three years; while Gregory retreated to Salerno, where he was protected by the Norman Duke of Calabria. Rome was taken, and Heinrich crowned Kaisar by the Antipope. Gregory VII. died while among the Normans, his last word being, "I have loved righteousness, and hated iniquity; therefore do I die in exile." His successor, Urban II., went on the same system of keeping the Church above all temporal power.

For a little while Heinrich triumphed, but his enemies stirred up his sons against him. Konrad, the elder, died at war with him; Heinrich, the second, actually stripped his father of his robes, and, in spite of his tears and entreaties, forced him to sign his abdication. Then the old man wandered about half-starved, and came to the Bishop of Speyer to entreat for some small office about the cathedral, but this could not be, as he was excommunicated, and he had even to sell his boots to buy bread! He died at Liège, in **1106**, and his body was put in a stone coffin in an island on the Maas, and watched day and night by a hermit till **1111**, when Heinrich V. came to an agreement at Wurms with the Pope that, though bishops should do homage for the lands they held of him, the King should not deliver to them the ring and staff, which betokened spiritual power. After this Heinrich IV. was buried. Heinrich V. died three years later. He had married our Henry the First's daughter Matilda, whom we call the Empress Maude.

CHAPTER XI.

LOTHAR II., ... 1125–1137.
KONRAD III., ... 1137–1152.

WHEN Heinrich V. died, without children, the Franconian line of Emperors came to an end, and ten great nobles from the four chief dukedoms met at Mainz to choose a new king. Heinrich had left all his own lands to his sister's sons, Konrad and Friedrich of Hohenstaufen, and one of these hoped to be elected; but the Germans feared that they would bring them as many troubles as had arisen under the last Franconians, and therefore chose in their stead Lothar, Duke of Saxony.

He thought he could never do enough to avoid the evils that Heinrich IV. had brought on the country, and so he asked Pope Innocent II. to ratify his election, and gave up the agreement at Wurms, with all rights to homage from bishops. This displeased the Hohenstaufen, and all who held for the power of the kings, and there was again a great war. The chief supporter of the King was Heinrich the Proud, Duke of Bavaria, who married his daughter Matilda, and was made Duke of Saxony. Heinrich's family was descended from a forefather named Welf, or Wolf, a Christian name often used, but of which a very odd story was told. It was said that the Countess of Altdorf laughed at a poor woman who had three children born at the same time, and that, as a punishment, she gave birth to twelve sons in one day. She was so much shocked that she sent all of them but one to be drowned in the lake, but on the way the maid, who was carrying them in her apron, met the count. He asked what she had there. "Whelps," she said; but he pulled aside her apron, and, seeing his eleven little sons, had them safely brought up, and they were known by the name of Welfen. One of the Welfs married into the Italian house of Este, and both in Italy and Germany the party of the Pope came to be known as Welfs, or Guelfs; while the party of the Kaisar were termed Waiblinger, from the castle of Waibling belonging to the Hohenstaufen. The Italians made this word into Ghibellini; and for many years there were fierce quarrels between the

Guelfs and Ghibellines, the first upholding the power of the Church, the second that of the State.

These kings of Germany were much less powerful than the great Emperors of the house of Saxony and Franconia had been; and now that all fiefs had been made hereditary, the great dukes and margraves were more independent of them, while the counts and barons (Grafen and Freiherren, the Germans called them) were likewise more independent of their dukes. Every one was building castles and fortifying cities, whence the nobles made war on each other, and robbed those who passed on the roads. There is a story of a Bishop who gave a knight the charge of his castle, and when he was asked how those within it were to live, pointed down the four roads that met there, to indicate that the travelers were to be robbed for the supplies! The larger cities governed themselves by a council, and called themselves free Imperial cities, and these were the most prosperous and peaceful places both in Germany and Italy, for even bishops and abbots did not always so keep out of the fray as to make themselves respected. The minne-singers, love-singers, or minstrels could, however, go about from town to town and castle to castle singing their ballads, and were always safe and welcome.

Lothar II Leading the Pope's Horse.

The great Countess Matildia had left all her dominions to the Pope, and Lothar acknowledged this right of Innocent II., and crossed the Alps in order to be crowned Kaisar. There was an Antipope set up by the Ghibellines, who held the Church of St. Peter and the Castle of St. Angelo, and as Lothar could not drive him out, the coronation had to be in the Church of St. John Lateran. He came a second time to Italy to put down a great disturbance in Lombardy, taking with him Konrad of Hohenstaufen, to whom he had restored the dukedom of Franconia, and had made standard-bearer to the Imperial army. Konrad was a good and noble man, brave, courteous, and devout, and respectful to the clergy, especially the Pope, which was the more remarked as he was the head of the Ghibelline party. The head of the Guelfs, Heinrich the Proud, was as much hated as Konrad was loved, for his insolence to every one from the Pope downwards, and for his savage cruelties to the prisoners who fell into his hands; but his father-in-law the Emperor favored him, and gave him the Marquisate of Tuscany.

On the way home, Lothar II. was taken ill, and died in a peasant's hut in the Tyrol, in 1137.

Heinrich the Proud fully expected to have been

chosen King of the Romans, but he had offended most of his party, even the Pope himself, and Konrad was elected. There was a battle between Konrad and Heinrich's brother Welf, at the foot of Weinsberg, a hill crowned with a castle, on the banks of the Neckar, and in this "Welf" and "Waibling" were first used as war-cries. The victory fell to Konrad, and he besieged the castle till those within offered to surrender. All the men were to be made prisoners, but the women were to go away in peace, with as much of her treasure as each could carry. All Konrad's army was drawn up to leave free passage for the ladies, the Emperor at their head, when behold a wonderful procession came down the hill. Each woman carried on her back her greatest treasure — husband, son, father, or brother! Some were angry at this as a trick, but Konrad was touched, granted safety to all, and not only gave freedom to the men, but sent the wemon back to fetch the wealth they had left behind. The hill was called Weibertrue, or Woman's Truth; and in 1820 Charlotte, Queen of Wurtemberg,* with the other ladies of Germany, built an asylum there for poor women who have been noted for self-sacrificing acts of love. Hein-

* Daughter of George III.

The Women of Weinsberg.

rich the Proud was reduced, and his two dukedoms taken away, Bavaria being given to Leopold, Margrave of Austria, and Saxony to Albrecht* the Bear, already Count of the Borders; but when Heinrich died, Konrad gave back Saxony to his son Heinrich the Lion, and Albrecht the Bear became Margrave of a new border country beyond Saxony, called Brandenburg, which he conquered from the Wends.

Germany had had little to do with the first crusade as a nation, though the noble and excellent Gorttfried of Bouillon, Duke of Lorraine, had been its leader, and first King of Jerusalem. But when St. Bernard preached the second crusade, Konrad took the cross, and went with an army of 70,000 men. They went by way of Constantinople, and in the wild hills of Asia Minor were led astray by their guides, starved and distressed, and when the Turks set upon them at Iconium, there was such a slaughter that only 7000 were left. Konrad went on and joined the host of King Louis V. of France at Nicea, almost alone, save for the knights from Provence, who had joined the French army, and whom Louis sent to form a train for their own Emperor. Together they landed at Antioch and be-

*Nobly bright.

sieged Damascus, where Konrad showed great valor, and is said to have cut off the head and arm of a Turk with one blow of his sword. But they could not take the city, and, disgusted with the falsehood and treachery of the dwellers in the Holy Land, Konrad returned home, and died three years after, in 1152. He was the first Kaisar who used the double eagle as his standard.

CHAPTER XII.

FRIEDRICH I., BARBAROSSA, . . . 1157-1178.

KONRAD III. left a son, but as he was very young the good king had recommended the nobles to choose his nephew Friedrich as their king, hoping that as his father was a Hohenstaufen, and his mother Jutta a Bavarian, the breach between Welfs and Waiblings might be healed. Friedrich was thirty-two years old, brave, keen, firm, and generous, but fiercely proud, violent, and self-willed. He was a grand-looking man, with fair hair and blue eyes, and a tinge of red in his beard, which made the Italians call him Barbarossa.

He gave Heinrich the Lion, Bavaria as well as Saxony, formed Austria into a duchy instead of a mark county, and he also made Windislav of Bohemia a king instead of a duke. He married Beatrice, the heiress of the county of Burgundy, which meant Provence, with its capital Arles. Konrad had never been crowned Emperor, and thus had no power in Italy, so that the Lombard cities had grown very powerful, and were used to govern themselves; the nobles were like little robber kings in their mountain castles, and at Rome, a priest named Arnold of Brescia had stirred up the people to turn out the Pope, Adrian IV., an Englishman, and set up a Republic in imitation of the old Commonwealth.

Friedrich felt himself called on to set all this right. He came over the Alps, marched into Rome, seized Arnold of Brescia, and had him executed, and then was crowned Emperor by Adrian IV. The people of Lodi came to ask his help against the citizens of Milan, who had conquered them, pulled down the walls of their city, and forced them to leave their homes and live in villages. Friedrich wrote orders that Lodi should be restored; but the Milanese tore his letter to pieces, and threw it in the face of his messenger, and most of the Italian cities took their part. The Emperor blockaded them, and cut off the hands of any unfortunate peasant who was caught trying to bring them provisions. They surrendered at last, and he made them swear fealty to him, and left them

Friedrich I Refuses the Milanese Submission.

under a judge. But in a short time they rebelled again, declaring they would give themselves to the Pope instead of the Emperor. Adrian IV. was dead, and some of the Cardinals elected Alexander III., but the others and the Roman people chose another Pope, who called himself Victor IV. Friedrich called on both to appear before a Council which was to decide between them, but Alexander, knowing himself to be rightfully elected, replied by declaring that the Emperor had no right to summon the successor of St. Peter before a Council. So only the friends of Victor came to it, and declared him to be the true Pope. Alexander then excommunicated both Friedrich and Victor, and Friedrich came in great wrath over the Alps to overthrow the Pope and punish the Milanese, who had insulted both him and his Empress in every way. He blockaded the city again, and forced it to yield. Before the day of surrender, he sent his gentle wife Beatrice away, lest she should move him from his purpose, and then all the chief citizens were marched out with their thirty-seven banners and the great standard of the city, which had a car all to itself when it went out to battle, and was embroidered with a Crucifix, beside which stood the figure of St. Ambrose giving his blessing.

The banners were thrown in a heap, the trumpets over them, at the Kaisar's feet, the car was broken to pieces, and the unhappy people wept so bitterly that even Friedrich's stern warriors shed tears of pity.

He told the citizens that they should have such mercy as agreed with justice, and called a diet at Pavia to judge them. The diet decided that Milan ought to be broken up as Lodi had been, the wall thrown down, the ditch filled up, the people forced to live in villages, all two miles from the ruined city and from one another, and each with a German governor. The people took some of their property with them, but much was forfeited and plundered, and a tenth was given to the churches and convents of Germany. Köln had for its share what were thought to be the relics of the Wise Men from the East, whom the Germans thenceforth called the Three Kings of Köln. Friedrich then appeared at Pavia in his crown, which he had sworn never to wear again till Milan had been punished, and he showed much favor to all the Ghibelline cities of Lombardy. Then he marched to Rome, while Alexander fled to Benevento, but it was the height of summer, and a terrible pestilence broke out in his army, cutting down many of Friedrich's near

Faithfulness of Sieveneichen.

kindred and best advisers, and great numbers of the troops. He was forced to retreat into Lombardy, but he found the whole country in insurrection, guarding the passes of the Alps against him, and at Susa a party of armed men broke into his chamber at night, and he had only just time to escape by another door, while a faithful knight named Herman of Sieveneichen threw himself into the bed to receive the death-blow while his master escaped. However he was recognized, and though in their rage the Lombards were going to slay him, they respected his faithfulness, and he was spared.

Germany was up in arms, and Friedrich had to subdue the rebellious princes. He was a great ruler, and founded Munich and several other great towns at home; but in the meantime the cities of Italy had united with the Pope against him in what was called the Lombard League, and had founded the city of Alessandria in honor of it, calling it by the name of the Pope. Friedrich crossed the mountains to put down this rising, but the Lombards were stronger than he had expected, and in the midst of the struggle, at his greatest need, Heinrich the Lion, Duke of Saxony and Bavaria, refused his help, probably because he did not like fighting against the Church, but declaring that he was too old for the campaign, though he was only forty-five, while the Emperor was fifty-four. Friedrich met him at Chiavenna, and actually knelt before him in entreaty not to ruin his cause by leaving him, but Heinrich, though distressed at the sight, held to his purpose, and rode off with his vassals.

Without the Saxons, Friedrich had to fight a battle at Lugnano, where the Milanese standard again appeared in its car, and the Welfs gained a complete victory. Friedrich's horse was killed under him, and he was thought to be slain, so that the Empress Beatrice had put on mourning as a widow, before he appeared again at Pavia, having escaped on foot by by-paths.

He was forced to make peace, and went to meet the Pope at Venice, where the Doge, in full procession conducted him to St. Mark's Church, at the door of which Alexander awaited him with all the clergy. The Kaisar knelt to kiss the Pope's slipper, and muttered in Latin (it is said), "Not to thee, but to Peter," which the Pope hearing answered with, "Both to me and to Peter." It is also said that Alexander then put his foot on Friedrich's neck, quoting the promise — "Thou shalt go upon the lion and the adder;" but as another ac-

Friedrich Kneeling to Heinrich the Lion.

count says he shed tears of joy at the reconciliation, it is not likely that these insults passed between them. The question was then finally settled that Bishops might be named by the prince, but that the cathedral clergy should have the power of accepting or rejecting them, and that though their land may be held of the prince, their spiritual power comes only through the Church, and is quite independent of him. The Milanese were restored to their city, and Friedrich went home, going on his way to Arles, where he and Beatrice were together crowned King and Queen of Burgundy — namely, what is now called Provence — in 1178.

CHAPTER XIII.

FRIEDRICH I., BARBAROSSA (*contd.*),.... 1174–1189.
HEINRICH VI........................ 1189–1197.

WHEN Friedrich I. came back to Germany, he held a diet at Wurms, and summoned Heinrich the Lion, Duke of Saxony and Bavaria, to answer for his treason, rebellion, and many other crimes. One of these was that in the middle of the night, in time of peace and friendship, he had attacked the town of Veringen, where the bishop of Freising had great salt works, destroyed them and all the storehouses, and dragged away the makers to Munich.

The Duke would not come, saying it was his right to be judged only in his own country, so another diet was held at Magdeburg, but he would not come to that, nor to a third at Goslau, where he was put under the ban of the empire — that is, made to forfeit his fiefs and honors, and declared an outlaw, for ban means a proclamation. He had friends, however, and held out for a long time, but he was so fierce and violent that he offended them all, and the Kaisar pushed him very hard, and besieged his city of Brunswick. There his wife, who was Matilda, daughter to King Henry II. of England, was lying ill. She ventured to send to Friedrich to ask that some wine might be sent in for her use, and he answered that he had rather make her a present of Brunswick than disturb her. He was as good as his word, for he drew off his army, but he gained so much upon the Lion, that at last Heinrich came to the diet at Erfurt, fell on his knees before the Kaisar, and asked pardon

Friedrich raised him kindly, but told him he had himself been the author of all his misfortunes. He was judged to have forfeited his great dukedoms, but the Kaisar allowed him to keep the Dukedoms of Brunswick and Luneburg, on condition that he should spend three years in exile at the court of his father-in-law, King Henry of England. Brunswick has ever since continued to belong to his family, the house of Welf or Guelf. Part of Saxony was given to Bernhard of Anhalt, the son of Albrecht the Bear, in whose line it continued, and it is from these two houses of Brunswick and Saxony that our English royal family have sprung. Bavaria was given to Friedrich's friend, Otto of Wittelsbach.

Now that peace was made, Friedrich held a great festival at Mainz, where he knighted his sons and held a tournament, to which came knights of all nations, forty thousand in number. A camp with tents of silk and gold was set up by the river-side, full of noble ladies who came to look on, and of minne-singers, who were to sing of the deeds of the knights. The songs and ballads then sung became famous, and there was much more of the spirit of poetry from this time forward in Germany. The Kaisar, old as he was, took his full share in the tilts and tournaments, and jousted as well or better than his three sons.

Heinrich, the eldest of these sons, had already been chosen to succeed his father, and was the first prince who was called King of the Romans, while the Kaisar was alive. Friedrich planned a grand marriage for him. The Kings of Sicily, who were of Norman birth, had always been great friends of the Popes, and sheltered them when the Emperors drove them out of Rome, but the last of these, of

The Diet of Mainz

the right line, had no child, and had only an aunt named Constance, who had always lived in a convent, though it does not seem certain whether she was really a nun. Friedrich used to say that Italy was like an eel, which must be held both by the head and tail if you would keep it. He had the head, and hoped the son would get hold of the tail by marrying Constance. Her nephew, the King, agreed to the match, and Constance, who was thirty-four years old, was sent to meet her bridegroom at Milan with a hundred and twenty mules carrying her marriage portion. The Pope, Urban III., was very angry, and deposed all the Bishops who had been at the marriage, or at Constance's coronation, and fresh struggles were just beginning, when all Europe was shocked by the news that Jerusalem had been taken by the Saracens under Saladin.

The Pope and the Kaisar both laid aside their quarrels to do all they could to rescue the Holy City, and, old as he was, Friedrich prepared to go on the crusade. He took his two younger sons with him, and a great army, in which were Leopold, Duke of Austria, and Konrad, Markgraf or Marquess of Monserrat. Passing through Constantinople, they marched through Asia Minor, suffering much for want of food and water, but at Iconium, where with his uncle Konrad he had once suffered such a sore defeat. Friedrich, with his war-cry, "Christ reigns! Christ conquers!" so dashed on the enemy as to gain a glorious victory. But only a few days after, as he was bathing in the cold, swift river Kalykadmus, a chill struck him, and he sank into the rapid current. He was seventy years old when he was thus lost, in the year 1190. His body was found and buried at Antioch; but the Germans could not believe their mighty Kaisar was dead, and long thought that in the Kyffhauser cave in Thuringia he sat with all his knights round a stone table, his once red, but now white, beard growing through the stone, waiting till the ravens shall cease to fly round the mountain, and Germany's greatest need shall be come, when he will waken up, break forth, and deliver her.

Friedrich's second son and namesake fought bravely, but soon caught the plague, and died when only twenty years of age. The Duke of Austria and Marquess of Monserrat joined the other body of crusaders, led by the Kings of France and England, at Acre, but Konrad was killed by an Eastern assassin, and Leopold was affronted by King Richard wanting him to assist in building up the walls

Richard the Lion Heart and Heinrich VI.

of Ascalon, and left Palestine. In the meantime, the King of the Romans, Heinrich VI., had been fighting hard with Heinrich the Lion, who had come home from England resolved to win back what he had lost, but all in vain. His son Heinrich had been betrothed to Agnes, daughter to the Pfalzgraf Konrad, brother to Friedrich I., and when the house of Welf was ruined, she would not give up her love to marry the King of France. Her mother favored her, and sent a message to the young Heinrich to come to her castle in her husband's absence. He came in the disguise of a pilgrim, and the mother immediately caused them to be married. When her husband came home the next morning, she met him with—"My lord, a noble falcon came yesterday to your tower, whom I have taken!" The two presented themselves, the Pfalzgraf forgave them, and thus peace was made, and the old Lion soon after died.

Young Heinrich was thus able to interfere on behalf of his English uncle, Richard the Lion Heart, when he had been shipwrecked in the Adriatic on his way from the Holy Land, and while trying to pass through the Tyrol as a pilgrim had been seized and imprisoned by Leopold, and afterwards made over to the Kaisar. The Pope demanded the release of a crusader, whose person ought to have been sacred, and the Kaisar held a diet at Hagenau, at which Richard was called upon to defend himself from the charge of having murdered Konrad of Monserrat, betrayed the cause, and other crimes.

HEINRICH VI.

Richard spoke with such grandeur and dignity that even Leopold turned aside weeping, and the Emperor sprang from his throne and embraced him. After this his ransom was accepted, and he did homage to Heinrich VI. as Emperor of the West, receiving from him the promise of the kingdom of Arles to add to his duchy of Aquitaine.

Heinrich took his wife into Sicily on the death of her cousin Tancred, and they were there crowned; but he showed himself a harsh and cruel ruler, and very avaricious. He went back several times between Sicily and Germany, and caused his little son Friedrich to be elected King of the Romans, but he was everywhere hated. He was planning a war with the Eastern Emperor, when, after hunting all day near Messina in the heat of August, he took a chill, and died at the age of thirty-one, in the year 1194. The Sicilians rejoiced publicly at the death of their tyrant, and murdered all the Germans they could find in the country.

CHAPTER XIV.

PHILIP, ... 1198–1208.
OTTO IV., ... 1209–1218.

LITTLE Friedrich, the son of Heinrich VI., was only three years old. He had been chosen King of the Romans as soon as he was born, but the Welfs declared that the election of an unbaptized infant could not be good for anything, and that there must be a fresh choice.

On hearing this, Philip, Duke of Swabia, the only surviving son of Barbarossa, left his sister-in-law Constance to secure Sicily and Apulia to herself and her child, and hurried back to the diet. There the Waiblings declared that it was no use to try to elect an infant, and that if Philip wished to keep the empire in his family he must be himself elected. He consented, and was chosen at Muhlhausen by the Waiblings, but the Welfs met at Köln and chose

Otto, Duke of Brunswick, the son of Henry the Lion, and had him crowned at Aachen. Philip was crowned at Mainz, but only by the Savoyard Bishop of Tarentaise, and the same year the Empress Constance died when only forty-three years old, having had her little son Friedrich Roger crowned King of Sicily and Apulia, and placed him under the special protection of the Pope, whom she begged to become his guardian, and to watch over both his kingdoms and his education.

The Pope at that time was Innocent III., a very great man, whose chief object was to make the power of the See of Rome felt by all princes; and as the first Norman conqueror had asked the Pope to grant the power over Sicily, he considered the kingdom a fief of the Roman See, and took charge of it and of the little king, whom the Normans called the Child of Apulia.

Innocent at the same time thought it needful to pronounce between the three princes, who had all been chosen kings of the Romans — Friedrich, Philip, and Otto. He threw over the child's election at once, and likewise declared Philip's unlawful, but he saw no objection to Otto's, and Otto promised his full support and faithfulness to Rome, and to give up possession of Countess Matilda's inheritance.

Germany thus was divided between the two kings till, in 1208, at the marriage festival of his niece Beatrice and Otto, Duke of Meran in the Tyrol, Philip was stabbed in the throat — no one knows why, unless it was the deed of a madman or drunkard — by the Bavarian Pfalzgraf, Otto of Wittelsbach. Philip left only two little daughters, whose mother died of the shock a few days after. The bridegroom, Otto of Meran, promised Beatrice never to rest till he had revenged her uncle's death, and Otto of Wittelsbach was hunted down among some shepherds as he was playing with a ram, and his head cut off.

Otto of Brunswick offered himself for a second election, and gained it, promising to marry Philip's orphan daughter Beatrice, who at eleven years old was led into the diet, while Otto said — "Behold your queen! Pay her due honors!" and then committed her to the care of her sister Agnes, the Pfalzgrafin of the Rhine, while he went to Italy to be crowned, and to try to bring Lombardy to be at peace.

It is said that Innocent III. wept for joy at having to crown a Welf Emperor, but the German

Murder of Philip.

troops were unruly, helped themselves to whatever pleased them in the Roman shops, and at last a fight took place in the streets, in which many were killed on both sides. Also, when Innocent claimed the lands which Countess Matilda of Tuscany had left to the Church, the Kaisar refused to give them up according to his promises, and the quarrel having begun, he most unjustly laid claim to the kingdom of Sicily as having been cut off from the empire, and actually marched into the Abruzzi.

Young Friedrich, the Pope's ward, defended himself bravely in Sicily, and Innocent, justly angered at the grasping and faithlessness of Otto, excommunicated him, and called on all his subjects to renounce their allegiance. Otto was obliged to hurry back to Germany, where, to strengthen himself, he immediately married Beatrice of Hohenstaufen, but only a fortnight later the poor little bride was found dead, poisoned, it was supposed, by his enemies. Otto was always looked on as belonging to his uncles, the Kings of England, and thus Philip Augustus of France hated him as one of that race. Once, when a boy, Otto had been at Philip's court with his uncle Richard, who pointed him out to the King, saying that one day that boy might be Emperor. Philip laughed scornfully, and said—

"When that comes to pass, I will give him Orleans, Chartres, and Paris." When Otto was really Kaisar, he sent to put Philip in mind of his promise. Philip replied that Orleans, Chartres, and Paris were the names of three little puppies, now three old hounds which he sent to the Emperor! At this time Philip was the friend and champion of Innocent III., while King John of England, Otto's uncle, was with his kingdom under the interdict, and Otto was felt to be following him in his misdeeds, rather than acting as a Welf, faithful to the Pope.

Therefore Friedrich was encouraged to make an attempt on Germany, and received the Pope's blessing and recommendation to the German nation, but only on condition that if he succeeded he should give up Apulia and Sicily, for the Popes did not choose to have the Emperors holding both ends of the eel of Italy. Though only eighteen, Friedrich was married to Constance of Aragon, and had a little son named Heinrich, whom he carried to be crowned at Palermo before he set off for Germany.

He was welcomed by the Waiblingers in Lombardy, but he took no army with him, and climbed the passes of the Alps alone with a guide, so as to descend into his own duchy of Swabia, where the

people were glad to see him. At Constance the gates were shut when Otto wanted to enter the city, and all the south of Germany soon owned the Apulian child, as Otto called him. He then went to France, and made a league with Philip Augustus, who gave him twenty thousand marks towards his expenses. He took the sum with him to Mainz, and when his chancellor, the Bishop of Speier, asked where he would have it kept, he answered — " Nowhere. It is to be given to our friends ; " and at Mainz all the Waiblinger chose him as King, and paid him homage.

Otto was, however, still strong in Brunswick and Saxony, the old homes of his line, but he had mixed himself up in a fierce quarrel of the Duke of Brabant, the Count of Flanders, and the other border vassals, with Philip Augustus, and joined them in a great attack upon France. All France united against them, and in 1214 there was fought the terrible battle of Bouvines, in which Philip gained a complete victory. Otto was in great danger, alone among the enemy, when a French knight tried to cut him down with a battle-axe, missed him, but so wounded his horse that, mad with pain, it tore back with him to his own troops, and there fell dead. He was remounted, but he could not bring his troops back to the change, and was forced to ride off with them, Philip scornfully saying — "We shall see nothing more of him but his back," though in truth Philip was a much less brave man. Otto's power was broken, and he fled to Köln, where his second wife, Marie of Brabant, added to his troubles by gambling away vast sums at dice. Being unable to pay them, he rode away from a hunting party to Brunswick, and she followed as a pilgrim, and Köln opened its gates to Friedrich.

Otto lived four years longer in Brunswick, and on his death-bed sent his crown by the hands of his brother Heinrich to Friedrich. He was then absolved from his long excommunication, and died in 1218. He had no children, so that Brunswick and Luneburg went to his nephew Otto, the son of his brother Wilhelm, our Queen's ancestor.

CHAPTER XV.

FRIEDRICH II., ... 1218.

FRIEDRICH II., "the Apulian child," was a wonderfully able and brilliant man, brought up in all the old learning that was still kept up in the Italian cities by the greatest scholars of the world, and with all the fire and spirit of the House of Hohenstaufen, together with the keen wit of the Sicilian Normans. Bred in Palermo, he preferred Italy to Germany, and as soon as Otto was dead he set out to be crowned Kaisar at Rome, after having caused his young son Heinrich to be chosen as his successor.

His wife Constance was dead, and the little crusading kingdom of Jerusalem had again fallen to a little girl, Yolande de Brienne, whom Friedrich married, undertaking, as King of Jerusalem, to lead a grand crusade to deliver the Holy City, which was still held by the Saracens.

The Pope, Honorius II., was not pleased with the marriage, and taxed Friedrich with breaking his promise of preventing Sicily from being in the same hands with Germany, since he had caused his only son to be elected to both: but Friedrich answered that he would take care to settle that, and went on into Sicily, where he had hard work in dealing with his fierce barons, and likewise with a colony of Saracens who had settled in the mountains and on the sea-shore, and gave much trouble to his people by land and sea. Friedrich conquered these Saracens, and moved them into the Apulian cities of Lucera and Nocera, treating them so kindly that he won their hearts, and they served him faithfully, but the Italians were angered by his bringing them among them. There was at this time much curious learning among the Saracens, especially in mathematics and chemistry. Friedrich delighted in such studies, and this raised the report that he was half a Saracen himself. Moreover, he was not leading the life of a good Christian man, but was giving himself up to all sorts of vice and luxury at Palermo. The Pope urged him to begin his crusade, and he sent for his vassals from Germany to join him in it.

Among them came the Markgraf Ludwig of Thuringia, a young man still, who had been married ever since he was a little child to Elizabeth, the daughter of the late King of Hungary. The two children had been brought up together at the castle of the Wartburg, and loved each other dearly, though Ludwig's mother, brother and sister hated and despised Elizabeth after her father was dead, and tried to set Ludwig against her pious and saintly ways, calling her the gipsy because she was dark complexioned, and the nun because of her prayers. Ludwig loved her through all, and upheld her in all her works of charity, when she nursed the sick, and laid them in her own bed, and fed orphan children, and went to the houses to feed the bedridden and dress their sores. There was a story that once, when he met her coming out of the castle with a heavy basket full of broken meat, he asked her what was there. She smiled, and bade him look, and it was full of roses. Perhaps this was meant to show how sweet are deeds of love, for Elizabeth never deceived him, nor did he find fault with her charities. Both were still very young when he was called to go on the crusade, and great was his grief at parting with her and his little children. With him went the chief German minne-singer of the time, Walter of Vogelwiede, and great numbers of noble knights, but the force could not be collected quickly, and those who came first had to wait, in the full heat of the summer, at Otranto and Brindisi to embark, till sickness began among them, and when at last they did embark it only became worse. Ludwig of Thuringia saw white doves flying round his mast — the sure sign of death in his family — and died before the fleet turned back, as it was forced to do, the Kaisar himself being very ill.

The Pope, Gregory IX., who knew Friedrich's proud character and evil, self-indulgent life, could not believe he had been in earnest about the crusade, and was too angry and impatient to inquire whether his illness was real or only an excuse, would not hear his messengers, and excommunicated him. Friedrich was very angry at the injustice, and it drove him further towards unbelief, and love of all the Church condemned, but he still went on with his crusade, though, before he sailed, his wife, Yolande of Jerusalem, died at the birth of her first child, who was christened Conrad. The Pope did not approve of this expedition being led

Friedrich II Putting on the Crown of Jerusalem.

by one who was still excommunicate, and forbade the Knights Templars and Hospitallers to follow his standard; but instead of fighting he made a treaty with Malek el Kameel, the Saracen Sultan, by which he made a ten years' truce, arranged that the pilgrimage to Jerusalem should be made safe, and that the Holy City should be put into his hands, with all its churches, the Moslems only keeping for themselves the Mosque of Omar, on the site of the old Temple. But the Pope's friends thought the treaty only a snare to get Christians into the hands of the Mahometans, and when Friedrich marched to Jerusalem, the Holy City was laid under an interdict while he should be there. No Holy Communion, no Church services took place when he visited the Church of the Holy Sepulchre, and he took the crown of Jerusalem off the altar, and crowned himself with it with his own hands. Then he came back to Italy, having learned in the East much of the old Greek learning which had passed to the Saracen Arabs, and, in especial, an Arabic translation of the Ethics of Aristotle, which was afterwards much studied in Europe.

The Pope had in the meantime caused Jean de Brienne, the father of Friedrich's late wife, to raise an army, and seize Apulia and Sicily in the name of his infant grandson Konrad, to whom Friedrich was bound, the Pope said, to have delivered it up. His soldiers were called the Key-bearers, as being sent forth by the See of Rome, and bearing the Keys of St. Peter made in cloth on their shoulders; but they were really only savage, plundering men-at-arms, and the people of the country all joined their Emperor gladly in expelling them. The Pope on this gave up his attempt, and peace was made between him and the Emperor, in which Gregory declared that the treaty with the Sultan was the best that could have been made, and absolved Friedrich.

The two had a conference at San Germano, but only one thing is known, that was there settled. The Germans had formed an order of soldier monks like the Templars and Hospitallers for the defence of the Holy Sepulchre, but as there were jealousies between the three, Friedrich wished the Germans, who were called Teutonic Knights, to be removed from the Holy Land, and set to fight with the heathen Sclavonians in the lands near the Baltic called Borussia (near Russia) or Prussia. Their Grand Master, Herman von Salza, was made a prince of the empire, and they were to have all the lands they conquered.

Friedrich stayed on in Italy, attending to a university he had founded at Naples, to which he invited scholars from all parts, especially the famous Scotsman, Michael Scott, who translated into Latin his Arabic version of Aristotle, and was looked on by all the ignorant as a great magician. The greatest scholar who grew up at Naples was St. Thomas Aquinas, a most wonderful teacher, who turned Aristotle's arguments to teach Christian truth. Friedrich's court was full of learning, elegance, and poetry, but chiefly of a self-indulgent kind. He so loved minstrelsy that he gave the city of Orange, in his kingdom of Arles, to a troubadour. The minne-singer Walther of Vogelwiede died about this time, and left lands whose produce was to be given to feed his fellow-minstrels the birds at his tomb, that so there might always be their sweet music round him.

It was a time of very great beauty in everything — poetry, dress, buildings, and all. One of the loveliest buildings in Germany is Marburg Cathedral, which was built by Konrad of Thuringia, brother of Ludwig, in memory of the "dear saint Elizabeth." When the news of Ludwig's death had come home, Konrad and his mother had driven her out with her five babies, homeless and wandering, and seized the goverment, but the barons and knights restored her little son. The Emperor wished to marry her, but instead of listening to his messages she went into a convent, where her confessor made her use hard discipline with herself, and she died when only twenty-four years old. Then her brother-in-law repented, and built this exquisite church in memory of her. This was the time too when the two orders of friars founded by St. Francis and St. Dominic were trying to teach people to love the world and its delights less, and to turn all their learning to holiness and the love of God.

CHAPTER XVI.

FRIEDRICH II., 1250.—*Concluded.*

FRIEDRICH II. had been 15 years absent from Germany since he set out after his election at Mainz. His eldest son, Heinrich, who had been chosen King of the Romans in his infancy, was sent to reign in Germany, even as a mere child, under the care of Ludwig, Duke of Bavaria, but there was so much crime and misrule that in the Dukedom of Westphalia Bishop Engelbert revived a strange secret tribunal called the Vehmegericht of Vehm, which is said to have dated from ancient rites around the Irmansul. Members were sworn in secretly, and met at night. Judges were chosen from among them, and before them persons were tried for their crimes, and if found guilty were sure to be found hanging on trees, a dagger stuck beneath, and the letters carved, S. S. G. G. (stock, stone, grass, green), the meaning of which no one knew. This Vehme was much dreaded, and did much good in keeping down evil-doers, when the regular courts of law were weak.

As Heinrich grew up he became discontented, and thought his father ought to resign the empire to him, and only keep Sicily and Apulia. The Duke Ludwig of Bavaria was murdered while taking an evening walk on the bridge of Kelheim, it is said, by an idiot, whom he had teased, but the young king declared that it was by one of the Eastern assassins sent by his father, and Friedrich and his people suspected Heinrich himself.

So many complaints were sent to the Emperor that he summoned his son and the German princes to a diet at Ravenna, and there tried to set matters straight between them, intending to come back to Germany as soon as he had arranged the affairs of Lombardy, but before he could do so Heinrich broke out into open rebellion, assisted by his brother-in-law, Friedrich, Duke of Austria, and laid siege to Wurms. The Kaisar again crossed the Alps, and being joined by all the loyal Germans, soon crushed the rebellion, and forced Heinrich to come and ask pardon. This was at once granted, but the wretched young man was found to be trying to poison his father, and was therefore sent

as a prisoner to Apulia, and was moved about from castle to castle there until his death.

Friedrich remained in Germany, and took as his third wife, Isabel, the sister of Henry III. of England, sending a splendid embassy to betroth her, and going to receive her himself at Wurms, where they were married in presence of four kings and eleven dukes, all sovereign princes. The festivities are said to have been even more splendid than those at his grandfather's diet at Mainz, and her English attendants were infinitely amazed by the elephants and camels which Friedrich had brought from the East.

Friedrich was called back to Italy by another disturbance in Lombardy, where the cities, with Milan at their head, had formed a league against him. He caused his son Konrad to be elected King of the Romans, and crossed the Alps with his army, and, being joined by all the Ghibellines in Northern Italy, he beat the Milanese at Corunuova. They hoped at least to have saved their beloved standard, but there had been heavy rain, the car stuck fast in a bog, and though they tried to carry off its gilt cross and ornaments, the Germans came too fast upon them, and they were forced to leave it in all its beauty. Friedrich had it drawn into

Rome in triumph by an elephant, and placed in the Capitol; but the war was not ended, for Friedrich required the Lombards to submit without making any terms, and they chose rather to defend themselves from city to city.

They knew that the wishes of the Pope were for them, for the Pope was displeased at Konrad, the heir of Sicily, being made king of the Romans, so that the southern kingdom would be joined to the empire, contrary to the Emperor's promise. There was another younger son of Friedrich named Heinrich, but called in German Heinz, and in Italian Enzio, a very handsome youth of twenty, whom Friedrich married to Adelais, the heiress of Sardinia, and made king of that island. But Sardinia had belonged to Countess Matilda, and Gregory declared it was part of the inheritance of the Church, and could not be given away.

On the very Palm Sunday of 1239 that Friedrich was holding a great tournament at Padua, Gregory excommunicated him again, and accused him of having uttered a most horrid blasphemy. This he denied with all his might, sending in his confession of faith, which agreed with that of all the Christian Church, though there is no doubt that he had a careless, witty tongue. The Pope did not consider that he had cleared himself, and tried to find an Emperor to set up against him; but St. Louis of France did not think he was fairly treated, and would not let any French prince be stirred up to attack him.

In the meantime things were going badly in Germany. Young Konrad was learning the German vice of hard drinking, and not making himself respected; and a horrid Mogul tribe, like the Huns of old, were overrunning Germany, and doing terrible damage, till they were beaten on the banks of the Danube. This stopped them, and though they laid Hungary waste, they did not venture again into Germany.

Gregory summoned a council of the Church of Rome to consider of the Emperor's conduct. The chancellor, Peter de Vineis, tried to persuade the German clergy not to go, telling them that at Rome they would find "broiling heat, putrid water, bad food, swarms of gnats, air so thick that they could grasp it, and a disgusting and ferocious race of men; that the Pope would be too cunning for them, and that their lives, their goods, and their souls would all be in danger." A great many were stopped by this, and as to the rest, Friedrich had a fleet on the Mediterranean, and had twenty-two shiploads of

Bishops and priests seized and carried to Naples, where it is said that he caused his chief foes among them to be put to death by hunger, and all were roughly handled and robbed, though the French and English were sent home in safety.

Gregory IX., who was nearly a hundred years old, died soon after this failure ; the next Pope lived only seventeen days, and Innocent IV., who was next elected, though hitherto the Emperor's friend, could not but go on with the old policy of the Popes taking the part of the Lombard league, and trying to reduce the power of the Emperor. As Friedrich said, when he heard of the election, he had only lost a friend, for no Pope could be a Ghibelline.*

There was an attempt to make peace, but it only made the breach wider, and Innocent fled from Rome to Lyons, which did indeed belong to the empire, but was much more out of Friedrich's reach than Rome, and then he called another council, to which the bishops could come by land. There all the Emperor's offences were again brought up against him, and he was again excommunicated and deposed. When he heard of it he had all his crowns

---

* Welfs and Waiblings in Germany, Guelfs and Ghibellines in Italy.

placed before him, and smiled as he said — "These are not lost, nor shall be till much blood has been shed."

St. Louis tried to make peace, but in vain. A few Guelf bishops were persuaded to elect Heinrich of Thuringia, brother-in-law of St. Elizabeth, but he was defeated, and died of his wounds. Then Wilhelm, Count of Holland, was set up, Friedrich struggling all the time against the Guelfs, both in Germany and Italy, with the help of Enzio of Sardinia, and Manfred, the son of his last wife, Bianca di Sancia, and his favorite among all his children. But while he was ill at Capua, he was warned that his physician had been bribed by his chancellor, Peter de Vigni, whom he had always trusted, to poison him in a draught of medicine. He bade the doctor drink half before his eyes. The man stumbled, and let most fall out of the cup. The rest was by Friedrich's orders given to a condemned criminal, who died of it at once. The chancellor was then imprisoned and blinded, and in the agony thus caused, dashed his head against the wall. Friedrich was bitterly grieved at such treachery in one whom he had so trusted. His son Enzio was made prisoner by the citizens of Bologna, who would not ransom him; and when St. Louis was taken prisoner by the Sultan in Egypt, the Pope accused Friedrich of having betrayed him. This accusation seems to have grieved Friedrich more than anything that had gone before. He was an old man, his strength was worn out, and his last illness came on at Luceria. His son Manfred attended to him, and the Archbishop of Palermo absolved him, and gave him the last sacraments before his death on Christmas-day, 1250. He was a great and noble, but not a good man, though he would have been far better if those who ought to have cared for soul, had **not** cared for power more than for their duty.

CHAPTER XVII.

KONRAD IV., ... 1250–1254.
WILHELM . . . . 1254–1256.
RICHARD, ... 1256–1257.

KONRAD had already been crowned King of Germany as well as King of Apulia and Sicily, and his father had decreed that Manfred should act as viceroy of the latter countries, desiring also that any lands taken from the Papal See should go back to it. But Innocent IV. would not acknowledge Konrad, and gave all his support to Wilhelm of Holland as King of Germany; while he made a present of Sicily and Apulia to little Edmund, the second son of Henry III. of England, undertaking to conquer it for him if the English would send him money. This they did, but Manfred was too strong for the Papal troops, and kept the kingdoms for his brother.

Konrad was very nearly murdered in his bed at

Regensburg, and the Count of Eberstein, who took his place while he escaped, was actually killed. He was a grasping, haughty man, not much liked, and he offended Manfred by harshness to his mother's relations. In a great battle at Oppenhein Wilhelm gained the victory, and Konrad soon after died of a fever, when only five-and-twenty, in the year 1254. His wife was Elizabeth of Bavaria, and she had one little son named Konrad, but who is generally called Conradin. She knew there was no hope of getting any of the kingdoms of his family for him while he was still a child, so she took him to her father's court, and begged the Pope to adopt him, as Friedrich II. had been adopted; but Innocent would not accept any of the House of Swabia, and the Guelfs were all of the same mind. Enzio had tried to escape from prison, but a tress of his long golden hair caught in the lock of the door and betrayed him, so that he was pursued, and brought back to die in captivity; and Manfred, who was crowned King of Sicily and Apulia, was conquered and slain by Charles, Count of Anjou, to whom the Pope gave away the two kingdoms.

Germany was in a most disturbed state, for Wilhelm was only half owned as King of the Romans. The most noted act of his life was the laying of the first stone of the splendid Cathedral of Köln, but he was so much disliked that the men of Köln set the house where he was sleeping on fire, in hopes of destroying him; and his own vassals, the Frieslanders, rose against him. It was winter, and he hoped to cross the ice to put them down, but as he was crossing a swamp the ice gave way under his horse's feet, and while he was struggling in the frozen mud, the Frieslanders came up and slew him without knowing him, in January, 1256. During all these wars the power of the King in Germany had been much lessened. The great dukes and prince bishops seized on one claim after another till, within their own lands, they became like kings and Friedrich II., by what was called a Pragmatic Sanction, had confirmed their rights, because he needed their help in his wars against the Pope and Lombard League. Also these princes had quite left off calling on any of the nobles or people to take part in choosing their king, and the seven chief among them always elected him. They were the three grand chancellors of the empire, being the Archbishops of Mainz, Köln, and Trier, with the King of Bohemia, grand cup-bearer; the Duke of Bavaria, high steward; the Duke of Saxony, grand marshal, and the Pfalzgraf of the Rhine. These were called electors, in German Kürfursten, and in the diet sat apart as a separate house or college.

Not only had the princes and nobles grown powerful in the absence of the Emperor, but the cities had become very strong. Many of them had trades and manufactures, and they governed themselves by their own town councils, training their men to arms, and fortifying themselves so as to be a match for the nobles. Those who owned no lord but the Kaisar called themselves free Imperial cities, and made leagues together to defend one another. The most famous of these leagues was called the Hansa —nobody quite knew why—and took in eighty towns, of which Lubeck and Hamburg were among the chief. They had fleets and armies, made treaties, and were much respected. Every citizen in these cities was trained to work at a trade. First he was an apprentice, then a journeyman; after that he was sent out for what was called his wander-year, to visit other towns and improve himself in his art, and on his return he might be sworn into the guild of his trade and be a master workman, who could be chosen to be a guild-master or burgomaster, and sit in the town council, which met in the beautiful Guild Hall or Rath-haus. The guilds formed trained bands, which went out to war under the banner of their craft, and the widows and orphans of those who died young were well taken care of. These cities, too, built splendid cathedrals, such as Ulm, Augsburg, Strasburg, and many more. In these cities there was some order during the evil days that followed Friedrich's death.

When Wilhelm perished, Konrad of Hochstatten, Archbishop of Köln, advised the other electors to choose a rich prince who could give them great rewards, and yet who should have no lands within Germany, so that he could not be able to subdue them all, and keep them in check. The brother of Henry III. of England, Richard, Earl of Cornwall, was pointed out to him as the best person, having immense wealth from the tin mines of Cornwall, and being connected with the empire through his wife, Sancha of Provence. Richard, glad of the honor done him, sent thirty-two wagons, all filled with gold, to buy the votes of the electors; but Arnold of Isenberg, the Elector Archbishop of Trier, was jealous of his brother of Trier, and set up as a candidate Alfonso X., King of Castille, whose mother was daughter to the murdered King Philip of Hohenstaufen. At Frankfort, on the 13th of January, 1257, Richard was chosen King of the Romans by four electors, and on the 1st of April

Alfonso was chosen by three, and the two candidates agreed that the Pope should decide between them; but he put off doing so year by year, and in the meantime both princes and towns grew more independent, and the cities in Italy ruled themselves, and almost forgot that the Emperor was their master.

Alfonso was called in his own country the Emperor, but he never came to Germany. Richard did try to do something for his own cause, and spent vast sums in gifts to the Germans. He made three visits to Germany, and was crowned at Aachen. where he kept court till he had to go and aid his brother in his struggles with the English barons, and there was made prisoner at Lewes.

In the meantime young Conradin had grown up to man's estate, and a party of Italians, who hated Charles of Anjou, invited him to come and win his father's crown. He set forth with his friend, Friedrich of Austria, and an army of Swabians and Bavarians. He was only twenty, very handsome, winning, and graceful, and all the Ghibelline Lombards joined him with delight. The Pope, Clement V., forbade him to proceed, and excommunicated him, but remained at Viterbo, while Conradin was welcomed at Rome, and his path strewed with flowers.

Then he went on to Apulia, but Charles had already crushed his friends there, and in a terrible battle at Sarcola routed his army. Conradin and Friedrich rode off, and meant to renew the fight in Sicily, but they were betrayed to Charles by a noble whom they trusted. The King collected a court of judges, who at his bidding condemned the two young men to death as robbers. Only one of all was brave enough to declare that such a sentence would be a murder, and he was not heeded. The two friends were tried and condemned to death without a hearing, and were playing at chess when they were told they were to die the next day. They prepared with great firmness and tender affection, and were taken to a scaffold on the sea-shore of the lovely Bay of Naples, in front of a church, Charles sitting at a window where he could see the execution. The sentence was read, and Conradin spoke a few words, owning himself a sinner before God, but, in challenge of his innocence toward man, he threw down his glove among the people. With a commendation to his Father in heaven, and a cry of sorrow for his mother, he laid his head on the block and died, and Friedrich, bursting into tears for his friend, was executed the next moment. The cruel deed was done in 1266.

CHAPTER XVIII.

RODOLF, ... 1278.

THE German princes enjoyed the freedom from all higher authority that arose from their having two absent foreign rival kings, but Germany was in a dreadful state of confusion, and bad customs sprang up which lasted for several centuries. Fist-right, which really meant the right of the strongest, was the only rule outside the cities, and even the bishops and great abbots were often fierce fighting men. The nobles lived in castles perched on rocks like eagles' nests, and often lived by plunder and robbery, and if two families had a quarrel, one chief sent the other a letter, called a feud-brief, giving a list of all the wrongs he considered himself or his people to have undergone, and defying the other and all his kindred, after which, each party was free to do the

German Castle.

other all the harm in his power. It was said that no noble cared to learn to write except to sign a feud-brief.

All the learning and civilization that the great Saxon and Swabian Kaisars had brought in was passing away, except in the cities. The nobles were growing more of boors, and giving way to their great vice—drunkenness, and Germany was falling behind all other nations in everything praiseworthy. If an enemy had come against the country it must have been overcome, and Ottokar, King of Bohemia, was so powerful as to be very dangerous. So when Richard of England died in 1271, the Pope, Gregory X., finding that no king was chosen, sent the electors word that if they did not choose a king he should send them one. Thereupon they chose Count Rodolf of Hapsburg. He was a good and brave man, whose possessions lay in Elsass, on the Swiss border, and had fought bravely under Ottokar against the Magyars of Hungary. He was very devout, and it was told of him that once when he was riding to Baden he met a priest on foot carrying the Holy Eucharist to a dying man over miry roads and torrents. He placed the priest on his steed and led him on his way, and when the sick man's house was reached, and the priest would have restored the horse, he said, "God forbid that I should ever again ride to battle the beast that hath carried the Body of my Lord," and he gave it to be used by priests going to visit the sick as long as it lived.

After a battle in which he lost his horse, the man who had killed it was about to be put to death but, he saved him, saying, "I saw his courage. So brave a knight must not be put to death."

Rodolf was fifty-five years old when he was chosen to be King of Germany, and a better choice could hardly have been made. When he was crowned at Aachen, no one knew what had become of the sceptre, but he took the crucifix from the Altar and made his oath upon it instead, saying that the symbol of redemption was a fit rod of justice. Gregory X. came to meet him at Lausanne, and kneeling before him, he promised obedience to the See of Rome, where he was to be crowned the next year. Ottokar, King of Bohemia, would not now even acknowledge him, and thought himself quite able to make himself independent. He had seized Austria when its Duke Friedrich died with Conradin, had robbed the poor youth's mother of Styria and had bought Carinthia, all without sanction from the Diet, and he was a terrible tyrant to all under him.

All Germany took part against him, and he was obliged to give up Austria, Styria, and Carniola, and come to do homage for Bohemia and Moravia in the island of Labau on the Danube. While he, in splendid array, was kneeling before Rodolf in his old grey suit, the tent over them was suddenly taken away, and all the armies behind them. Ottokar thought this a great insult, and as soon as he could raise his troops again, began another war, and there was a terrible battle at Marchfield, near Vienna, where Rodolf gained a great victory, and cut the Bohemians to pieces. He tried to save Ottokar's life, but the corpse was found pierced with seventeen wounds. Ottokar's Queen submitted, and his little son Wenzel remained King of Bohemia, but Austria, Styria, and Carniola were given by Rodolf to his sons Albrecht and Rodolf.

Rodolf tried to revive the power of the Empire over Tuscany and Lombardy, but he found that he was not strong enough; and rather than quarrel with the Pope, he gave up to Rome all that it had so long claimed of Countess Matilda's legacy. When he was asked why he did so, he said, "Rome is like the lion's den in the fable; I see the footsteps of many animals who go thither, but of none who come back."

He was very much beloved at home. He traveled through Germany listening to every complaint. When his men would have kept some peasants from coming near him, he said, "For Heaven's sake let them alone. I was not made King to be shut up from mankind." He always lived and dressed plainly, and when he heard some of his knights grumbling at the badness of the rye bread and sour wine he was sharing with them, he dismissed them from his service as too dainty for him.

At Mainz one winter morning he was walking about in his old grey dress, and turned in to a baker's shop to warm himself at the fire, but the woman crossly said, "Soldiers have no business in poor women's houses." "Be content, good woman," he said. "I am an old soldier, who have spent my all in the service of that fellow Rodolf, who still suffers me to want." "It serves you right," said the woman, and she began hotly to abuse the Kaisar, saying that she and all the bakers in the town were ruined by his means, and to get rid of him, she dashed a pail of water on the fire and smoked him out. When he sat down to his own dinner he ordered a boar's head and bottle of wine to be taken to the baker's wife as a present from the old soldier. Of course this brought in the woman, crying out for forgiveness, which he granted her, but on condition that she would tell the company all she had said of him. And as he put an end to much extortion on the part of the tax-gatherers, and made the country peaceful, so that the peasants could safely sow and reap, no doubt the bakers soon had no reason to complain. He destroyed sixty-six nobles' castles in Thuringia alone, and hung twenty-nine nobles at once at Erfurt, and was equally severe to ill-doers everywhere but not too severe, and the saying was, "He was the best warrior of his day; he was the truest man that ever won the office of a judge."

He had a large family, three sons and seven daughters, but one son was drowned, and the second, Rodolf, who was married to the daughter of King Ottokar, died in 1290, before the birth of his only child, Johann. After this, the Kaisar tried to have Albrecht, the only remaining son, chosen King of the Romans in his own lifetime, but the electors said they could not support two Kings at once, and put the matter off to another diet. Rodolf was seventy-four years old, and did not live to see that promised diet, dying on the 15th of July, 1291, at Germesheim, on the Rhine. He had never been actually crowned by the Pope, but was generally called Kaisar. He was one of the best rulers Germany ever had, and was the founder of the House of Hapsburg in Austria.

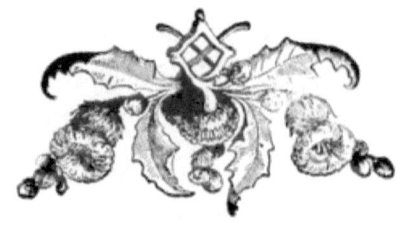

CHAPTER XIX.

ADOLF, ... , ... 1291–1298.
ALBRECHT, ...   1298.

GERHARD, Archbishop Elector of Mainz, persuaded the other electors to choose his kinsman, Adolf of Nassau, who is said to have been the poorest prince who ever sat on the throne of Germany. He was fierce and grasping, and made himself much hated.

When Edward I. of England was going to war with France he made an alliance with Adolf and offered him a sum of money to equip an army to gain back the kingdom of Arles. But Adolf spent the money in buying Meissen and Thuringia from the Landgraf Albrecht, called the Degenerate, who had misused his wife, Margarethe, the daughter of Friedrich II., and taken her children from her. When she parted with them, instead of kissing the eldest, she gave him a fierce bite on the cheek, that the scar might always remind him of her wrongs. The two boys tried to flee from their father, but were taken, and would have been starved in prison if the servants had not had pity on them, fed them, and set them free.

They soon found friends to reclaim the inheritance which their father had sold, and half Germany joined them, for Adolf's hired soldiers were detestably cruel. Once they caught two poor women, tarred them all over, rolled them in feathers, and showed them off in the camp as a couple of strange birds, and when the Count of Hohenstaufen complained to the King, he was rudely driven away. The two brothers were beaten in battle, but they kept their own inheritance, for the Thuringians defended themselves bravely for three years, and at the end of that time, Archbishop Gerhard was so ashamed of Adolf as to persuade the other electors that he had justly forfeited the Empire, and they chose Albrecht of Hapsburg, Duke of Austria, the son of the good Rodolf, in his stead.

There was a great battle near Wurms between Albrecht and Adolf. One history says that they met, and that Adolf cried, " Here you shall abandon to me Empire and life," to which Albrecht answered,

"Both are in the hands of God," giving him such a blow that he fell from his horse and was killed by some of the Austrians. His knights were so heavily armed that when once their horses were killed they could not get up but lay helpless, till some one came either to stab them or put them to ransom. This was in 1298.

Albrecht was elected over again and crowned at Aachen. He was very tall and grim-looking, and made the more frightful by the loss of an eye. His great desire was to use his power over the Empire to make his family great, and on the death of Wenzel, the last of the line of Bohemian kings, he obtained that his son Rodolf should be chosen to succeed him. Rodolf would not have been a bad ruler left to himself, but his father forced him to be so harsh that the Czechs rebelled, and when he died in the midst of the war with them, they declared they would rather have a peasant for their king than his next brother Friedrich, and chose Heinrich of Carinthia, the husband of the late King's sister.

Albrecht did one good thing, in forcing the Archbishop Elector of Mainz and the Pfalzgraf to lower the very heavy tolls they took from every one who sailed along the Rhine. Archbishop Gerhard, who viewed himself as a sort of king-maker, said he had only to blow his horn to call up as many Kaisars as he pleased; but Albrecht was too strong for him, and the Pope would not help him.

Next Albrecht attacked the Landgraf of Thuringia, Friedrich with the bitten cheek. Tidings came to the Wartburg that the King was coming with a large army, and the young Landgraf had to flee with his wife and their newly-born child. The little one began to cry violently when the enemy were almost overtaking them, and the Landgraf made his little troop stop, and kept the enemy at bay while his baby was fed and pacified. He was a giant in size and strength, as is shown by the suit of armor still preserved at the Wartburg, and his skill proved sufficient to drive out the Austrians, and save his inheritance.

Another attempt of Albrecht was to use his power as King of the Romans to make the mountaineers of Switzerland subject to his own dukedom of Austria. The three little cantons of Uri, Schwitz, and Unterwalden were bitterly grieved by the harshness of his governor, Gesler, who lived at Altdorf, in a castle which he called Zwing Uri (Force Uri), and three men, Furst, Melchtal, and Werner, met at night and swore to raise the country against the tyrants, each gaining secretly as many confederates as he could. According to the cherished Swiss story, the outbreak was brought on at last by Gesler's setting up his hat in the market-place at Altdorf, and insisting that all the peasants should make obeisance to it. When Wilhelm Tell, the best archer of Uri, passed it unheeding, he was seized and made to ransom his life by shooting an apple placed on his little son's head. He succeeded, but on being asked why he had another arrow in his belt, he answered that had he slain his child, he should have used it to pierce the bailiff's heart. Gesler in his rage declared that he should be placed where he would never see the sun or moon again, and was carrying him off in a boat across the Lake of Lucerne, when a tempest made it needful to unbind the only steersman who could save the lives of the crew. Tell brought the boat to shore, and then leaped ashore and fled. Watching his opportunity from behind a hollow tree, as the officers came in persuit of him, he shot Gesler dead, then rushed away to his comrades, who at once broke forth, seized several castles by surprise, pulled down Zwing Uri, and on the 6th of January, 1308, raised the banner of the Swiss Confederation, and prepared for defence.

The rising is certain, but great doubts exist as to

the story of Tell, which is found in no chronicle of the time, and which historical critics now declare to be an old story like that of Siegfried and the dragon at Wurms, only placed at a later time.

Albrecht swore to be revenged on the Swiss boors, and was collecting his forces when his nephew, Johann, the son of his brother Rodolf, came, as he had often done before, to demand possession of his father's inheritance, as he was now nineteen years old. Albrecht scoffingly threw him a wreath of flowers, saying those were the fit toys for his age. Johann vowed vengeance, and arranged his plan with four nobles whom Albrecht had offended. The king was on his way to Rheinfelden, and was in sight of the Castle of Hapsburg, when he had to be ferried over the river Reuss. Johann and his party managed to cross in the first boat with him, leaving the rest of his train on the other side of the river. Then, crying, "Wilt thou now restore my inheritance?" Johann stabbed him in the neck, and three of the others also struck; then all fled, and left him dying, with his head in the lap of a poor woman. They took refuge in Switzerland, but the confederates would have nothing to do with murderers, and the four nobles were given up to justice. The King's family insisted on their punishment being that most cruel one of being broken on the wheel. The one of the party who had not struck Albrecht, Rudolf von der Wart, shared the same horrid death, but was comforted and tended through all the long anguish by his faithful wife Gertrude. Johann the Parricide, as he was called, struck with remorse, after long wandering, came to the Pope, who gave him absolution, and he ended his life in a convent. Albrecht was killed in 1308.

CHAPTER XX.

HEINRICH VII., ... 1308–1313.
LUDWIG V., ... 1313–1347.

AT the time of Albrecht's death, Philip the Fair of France had forced Pope Clement V. to come to live at Avignon, and do his bidding in everything. Philip made Clement command the Electors to choose Charles, Count of Valois, his own brother, but they would not hear of another stranger. Nor would they hear of another king of the house of Hapsburg, but chose instead Heinrich, Count of Lützenburg, the little castle, more commonly called Luxemburg, who was brother to the Archbishop of Trier.

He had never thought of becoming King of the Romans, and was much amazed when the tidings reached him, but he set himself to fulfil his duties, and was one of the best men who wore the crown of Karl the Great. The four sons of Albrecht came to ask investiture of their father's hereditary dominions, and he advised them not to meddle with Austria, which, he said, had been fatal to five kings. They in return advised him not to be the sixth king to whom it should be fatal, and he ended by giving it to Friedrich, the eldest of them, on condition that Switzerland should be declared independent of the duchy, and that they should assist him in his plans as to Bohemia and Italy.

Heinrich of Carinthia had turned out a cruel tyrant, and the Czechs hated him. He had shut up Elizabeth, the sister of Wenzel, the last king of Bohemia, in a castle, whence they had delivered her, and then offered her to the King of the Romans for his son Johann. He easily drove out the Carinthian, and the marriage took place when the lady was twenty-two and her bridegroom fourteen. She was a wild, rough, uncivilized being, and Johann, who was a gentle, graceful, knightly prince, never was happy with her, and often left her to rule her own kingdom, while he joined any warlike enterprise that might be afoot.

Heinrich was resolved to restore the old power of the empire in Italy, and to free Rome from the interference of the French. In 1310 he crossed the Alps, and took the cities of Lombardy that tried to hold out against him, then went on to Rome, where he found the city divided between two factions, one who held for him, the other who were in the

MEDIÆVAL COSTUMES.

interest of the French, and had hoped to keep him out by the help of the French King's cousin,

Robert, King of Naples. Heinrich, however, gained the Capitol, the Colosseum, and the Church of St. John at the Lateran Gate, but he was repulsed from the Vatican and from St. Peter's. The Pope had been obliged to send three Cardinals with a commission to crown him, and this was done at the Church of St. John, but the enemy actually shot arrows into the choir, which fell on the altar while the Kaisar was kneeling before it. He soon after took his troops to Tivoli, to avoid the unwholesome summer air in Rome. He shewed much justice and wisdom, and the best Italians began to look on him as a perfect head to the State, such as they had always hoped for. He was going to invade Naples, because King Robert stirred up all the Guelfs in Italy against him, when he died suddenly on the 24th of August, 1313. One account says that a priest actually poisoned him with the sacred Chalice, of which Emperors partook in right of their consecration, and that, when he discovered what had been done, he said, "In the Cup of Life thou hast offered me death; fly before my people can take thee," and that his reverence for the holy Elements prevented him from using any means of saving his life. His grandson, however, declared that he did not believe the story. Any way, Germany and the Italian Ghibellines had a great loss in the good Kaisar Heinrich VII.

The electors met at Frankfort, each with an army of knights to support his choice. Five, with Johann of Luxemburg, King of Bohemia, at their head, chose Ludwig, Duke of Bavaria, whose mother was a daughter of Rodolf of Hapsburg, and the other two, Friedrich, Duke of Austria, son to his eldest son. Ludwig was crowned at Aachen, and Friedrich at Köln. Ludwig held most of the north, Friedrich most of the south. Neither could concern himself about Italy at all, and Germany fell back into horrid misrule and disorder, earthquake, famine, and pestilence making the distress much more dreadful. The Swiss, too, beat the Austrians in a terrible battle at Morgarten.

At last the two cousins fought a dreadful battle at Muhldorf in 1322. Friedrich thought the victory was his, when he saw a fresh force advancing, and supposed that it was a body of men led by his brother Leopold prepared to rejoice with him, but it proved to be a Bavarian troop, under one Sifred Schwepperman, who came suddenly down on the tired Austrians, mowing them down like grass. One family lost twenty-three members. Ludwig, who had thought himself beaten, was amazed when first young Heinrich of Hapsburg was brought to him as a prisoner, then the Duke of Lorraine, then Friedrich himself. That evening the steward came to say that he had nothing for the King's supper but eggs, and very few of them. "An egg a-piece," said Ludwig, "and two for faithful Schwepperman. If I sleep in my camp to-night, it is owing to Sifred!" These words were graven on Sifred's tomb, and an egg was blazoned on the family shield.

HEINRICH VII.

Ludwig received Friedrich with the words, "Sir cousin, you are welcome," and sent him to the Castle of Trausnitz, his brother Leopold still trying to maintain his cause. Pope John the XXII., still in Avignon, laid Germany under an interdict because Ludwig had been made King of the Romans without his sanction, but the Franciscan friars were on Ludwig's side, and continued to minister to the people. After three years, Ludwig came to visit Friedrich in his prison, and reminding him of their near relationship, proposed that they should reign jointly, both being called Kings of the Romans, and their signatures changing places every day. This was agreed to, and though the Pope dissolved the treaty, the two cousins held faithfully to it, but it did not save the life of Friedrich's brother Leopold, who had been pining to death ever since the battle of Muhldorf, grieving for not having come up in time.

Ludwig entered Italy, was crowned at Pavia with the iron crown, and set up a Pope of his own, who crowned him at Rome. Friedrich died in 1330, and Ludwig, as the only Kaisar, held a great diet at Reuse on the Rhine, where the princes declared the Roman Emperor to be the highest power on earth, and to be chosen only by the Electoral princes of Germany.

This became the law of the land, and Ludwig seems to have thought himself head of spiritual matters as well as temporal, for he dissolved the marriage of Margarethe Maultasch, or Wide-mouth, the heiress of the Tirol, with the second son of King Johann of Bohemia, and gave her to his own second son, Ludwig, whom he had made Markgraf of Brandenburg. This deed made good men, who had hitherto thought him hardly used, turn against him, and they were also jealous when he made another son, named Wilhelm, Count of Holland. He wavered too in his alliance with Edward III. of England, at one time making him his Vicar in the Low Countries, and then turning against him.

The electors met in 1344, and chose a new King of the Romans, Karl of Luxemburg, the

ADOLF.

eldest son of King Johann of Bohemia, and grandson to Heinrich, but the greater part of the country adhered to Ludwig, and in truth Karl was more French than German. His name was really Wenzel, but he had been sent in his youth to the court of his aunt, the wife of Charles IV. of France, who had given him his name, which is Karl in Germany, and his sister Gutha, or Bonne, as the French called her, was married to Jean, the heir of France. His election at first only turned the Germans against him, and he and his father, now blind, both left the country, and fought under the French standard against Edward III. at Crecy, where Johann was killed, and Karl fled from the field.

The next year, 1347, Ludwig of Bavaria died suddenly in the middle of a bear hunt.

CHAPTER XXI.

GUNTHER, ... 1347–1347.
KARL IV., ... 1347–1378.

KARL IV. was looked on in Germany as almost a Frenchman, and some of the Electors chose Count Gunther of Schwartzenburg in his stead. Gunther was a good old man and much respected, but he died immediately after his election, and it was thought that he had been poisoned. After attending his funeral in full state, Karl was crowned at Aachen.

The Pope much wished to get back to Rome from Avignon, but was afraid of getting under the power of Germany as he was now under that of France, so he very cautiously treated with Karl. A commission was sent to crown the Emperor at Rome, but only on his promise to stay there no longer than for one month, without arms or army:

a promise which the Ghibellines thought unworthy of one who called himself the Roman Emperor.

Karl was said to be the **father of Bohemia**, his hereditary kingdom, but the step-father of Germany. He sold the crown lands, and he also sold titles and honors to the nobles, thus greatly weakening future Kaisars, and adding to the power and lawlessness of the counts and barons, who heeded him little. Besides, the empire was visited by the Black Death, the horrible disease that raged all over Europe, and was specially dreadful in Germany, where whole villages were left without an inhabitant, and even the cats, dogs, and pigs died. People treated this visitation in different ways. One set declared it was owing to the Jews, and persecuted them frightfully, 2000 of them being burned in one pile in Strasburg alone. Others more rightly thought that the pestilence was a visitation for the sins of Christians, but supposed that penitence might best be shown by scourging themselves. An order called Flagellants was formed for the purpose, and men and boys, stripped to the waist, went through the streets in the towns singing litanies, while each beat the man in front of him with rods or scourges till he was streaming with blood. The wisest people were the women, chiefly in Flanders, who banded together, under the name of Béguines, to nurse and tend the sick.

In 1356 Karl held a great diet at Nuremburg, at which was drawn up the Edict that was called the Golden Bull, from the golden ball or bubble in which its seal is enclosed. It is a very noted document, for it fixed the constitution of the Kingdom of Germany and of the Holy Roman Empire, making seven Electors, three spiritual and four temporal, and declaring that each in his own province should be a sovereign prince, with no appeal from his decisions, except to the Kaisar himself. The three spiritual Electors were the Archbishops of Mainz, Köln, and Trier; the four temporal were the King of Bohemia, the Margraf of Brandenburg, the Pfalzgraf of the Rhine, and the Duke of Saxony. It was published in the presence of the Emperor on his throne, and the next year another diet was held at Mainz, at which each Elector was present, and feasted in the market-place, each in character with the office he bore in the Imperial household, the three Archbishops each with a seal hanging round his neck as Arch Chancellors, the Duke of Saxony with a silver peck of oats as Master of the Horse, the Markgraf of Brandenburg with a basin and ewer of gold as grand seneschal;

the Emperor's nephew, Wenzel, representing the Bohemian king as grand butler, brought wine in a golden flagon, and the Pfalzgraf of the Rhine, the grand carver, served up the dishes. After the banquet, the Margraf of Misnia and the Count of Schwartzenburg, as grand huntsmen, sounded their horns, called up their hounds. and killed a bear and a stag in presence of the Emperor. At this diet was present Charles, the Kaisar's nephew, and heir of France, who had just become Count Dauphin of Vienne. and was thus a vassal of the empire.

This Emperor founded the first German university at Prague, and further did all he could to adorn that city, and he was the first to discover the properties of the waters of Carlsbad, which still bears his name ; but he cared little for Germany, and bands of robbers were again infesting the whole country, and the Barons who held direct of the empire, without any Duke or Count over them, were especially violent and ferocious, making their castles on the mountain tops a terror to all around.

Karl, however, cared most for French and Italian affairs. A new Pope, Urban V., was resolved to return to Rome, and he had a warlike Cardinal, named Egidio Albornoz, who prepared his way by making the people submit to him. The Emperor met the Pope at Avignon, and was crowned by him King of Arles, before going to Lombardy, where the cities had grown so much used to governing themselves that few made him welcome, and those who did found him weak and treacherous, and ready to do anything. grant any favor, or break any promise, provided he was bribed.

However, when Urban arrived at Rome, Karl met him at the gates, and walked by his side on foot, leading his horse. When the Pope said Mass he served as a deacon, and he caused his fourth wife, Elizabeth of Stettin, to be crowned at Rome, after which he stayed four months in Tuscany, chiefly at Lucca, trying what he could get from the Italian cities, and the families who were trying to become their lords.

Urban was obliged to return to Avignon, and there died; but the next Pope, Gregory XI., really came back to Rome, though the Cardinals had come to dislike the city so much that six of them stayed behind at Avignon. When Gregory died in 1378, some of the Cardinals chose Urban VI., an Italian, who could be trusted to live at Rome, but some who longed to be back at Avignon declared that they had only done so because the Roman mob had been shouting round them, "A Roman, a Roman." They fled away, and chose a Pope of their own who would live at Avignon, and thus began the great

KARL IV.

schism which did much harm to the Church. England and Germany held with the Roman Pope, France with the Avignon Pope.

In that same year, 1378, Karl IV. died. He was a clever man, who knew many languages, and ruled Bohemia well, but he was careless of Germany, and used Italy as a mere treasure-house. By much bribery he had managed to get his eldest son, Wenzel, chosen King of the Romans two years before his death, and he had persuaded his brother to make him heir also to Luxemburg. He had another son named Siegmund, and his daughter Anne was our " good Queen Anne," the much-loved wife of Richard II.

CHAPTER XXII.

WENZEL. . . . . 1378–1400.

WENZEL or Wenceslaf of Luxemburg, King of Bohemia, had been chosen King of the Romans, and succeeded his father at seventeen. He was a man of rude and coarse nature, more like one of the half-crazed Roman Emperors than any Christian ruler in the strange, wild cruelties he committed. He left Germany to itself, and the disorders there grew so great that the cities, and the better sort of nobles in Swabia, formed themselves into a great league for defending one another and keeping order, sometimes attacking and taking robbers in their castles, and having them put to death. In truth, the king had now so little power in Germany that his ferocity could not do much mischief there. When he sent to the citizens of Rothemburg for a contribution of 4000 florins, and they refused, all the harm he could do them was to answer them in this letter, which is still preserved:

"To our unfaithful men of Rothemburg, who are disobedient to the Empire.

"The devil began to shear a hog, and spake thus, 'Great cry and little wool.' REX."

But at his own Court at Prague he could show what he was. He invited the Czech nobles to an entertainment, where they found three tents pitched, black, white, and red. Wenzel himself was in the black tent, and as each came in, demanded of him what crown lands he held. If the noble said he was willing to yield them up, he was taken to the white tent, where he found a sumptuous banquet; but if he declared that he had a right to them, he was hurried off to the red tent and beheaded.

At the next entertainment he gave, before his guests sat down, he showed them the executioner leaning on his axe, and said to that grim personage, "Wait awhile, thou shalt have work enough after dinner." The nobles were not slow to take the hint, and Wenzel got whatever he chose to demand of them.

His wife must have had a miserable life, for he kept a pack of bloodhounds always about him at table and in bed, where she was often torn by them.

This unfortunate lady was Johann of Bavaria, and she had a confessor named Johann Nepomuk, who led her to become very pious and devout, and could sometimes even restrain the King himself. Once, however, when a fowl had been served up underdone, Wenzel ordered the unhappy cook to be fastened to a spit and roasted before the fire. Nepomuk threw himself before him, and used every means to make him change his horrible sentence, but in vain. He was only ordered off to prison, and kept there for several days, after which he was sent to the palace, invited to dinner with the King, and treated with great honor. But when Wenzel was alone with him, he found that it was to make him tell what the Queen said to him in confession, and this, as a good priest, he could not do. The King finding persuasion and promises in vain, had him tortured, and as he still refused, he was thrown bound hand and foot into the Moldau in the middle of the night, from the bridge which still bears his name; but his corpse floated up, and was carried to the Cathedral, the clergy and people flocking to see and touch it, as that of a saint and martyr.

Wenzel's chief favorite was his executioner, whom he used to call "Gossip." He declared that

Arnold Von Winkelried.

he wanted to know what a man felt when he was beheaded, so he told the executioner to bind his eyes, laid his head on the block, and cried, "Strike." The man did so, but only with the flat of the sword. The King started up, ordered him to lay down his head in his turn, caught the sword up, and actually cut off his head!

His brother Siegmund, whom his father had made Elector of Brandenburg on the failure of the old line, and who had been married to the daughter of the King of Hungary, chosen by the Magyars as their king, was asked by the Czechs what to do with this dreadful madman. He advised them to keep him as a prisoner, and they shut him up in a castle at Prague. After some months, one day, when he was allowed to bathe in the Moldau, he managed to make his escape in a boat rowed by a young girl, and reaching one of his castles on the other side of the river, took up arms against the people. His brother Siegmund was called in, and coming with an army, made him prisoner again, and sent him to Vienna. There he was shut up in one of the towers of the castle, from the window of which he saw an old fisherman named Grundler giving alms, whenever he could, to the prisoners in the court. Wenzel called him, and so talked him over that he brought a silken cord, by means of which the King let himself down from the tower to a boat on the Danube, where Grundler was waiting to row him across. He reached Prague, and there set up his banner again, got back his kingdom, and rewarded Grundler by making him a noble.

In the meantime another attempt had been made by Duke Leopold of Austria to subdue the Swiss. He came with an army of 4000 knights against the peasants, who only mustered 1400 men, many of them with shields of wood, and clubs with spikes round their heads, which they called morning stars. A knight called Hans of Hasenburg (Hare Castle) begged the Duke not to fight till his infantry should have come up, but another knight cried, "Hare Castle! Hare Heart rather! I'll serve these fellows up to-night to the Duke, boiled or roasted, whichever he likes best."

The Austrians, who had sent their horses away because the ground was rough, drew up on foot at Sempach like one steel wall bristling with spears. The peasants knelt for a moment in prayer, and then an Unterwalden farmer, Arnold von Winkelried, shouted, "I will make a way for you, comrades. Take care of my wife and children." Therewith he dashed against the spears, grasped as many as he could in his arms, and pressing them all against his breast, held them there in the clasp of death, while the Swiss pressed into the gap he made, over his body, and broke the German ranks. Terror seized the army; they fled, all but the few braver ones, who fought hard and desperately. The Duke was among them, and was killed at last as he lay wounded on the ground by a hump-backed plunderer, who was hung by the Swiss for the cowardly murder. Wenzel had by this time grown entirely unbearable, and in 1400 a diet was held at Laenstein, which deposed him and elected Friedrich of Brunswick; but on the way to Frankfort to be crowned the

WENZEL.

new King was treacherously murdered by the Count of Waldeck. Then the Electors chose the Pfalzgraf Ruprecht of the Rhine, and Wenzel said he was very glad to hear of his own deposition, since he should have more time to attend to his own kingdom. He behaved much better during the nineteen years he survived, and took much interest in the University at Prague, where Johann Huss was the Professor of Philosophy, and taught the doctrines of Wickliffe, which had been brought from England by a noble in the suite of Queen Anne.

CHAPTER XXIII.

RUPRECHT, ... 1400–1410.
JOBST, ... 1410–1411.
SIEGMUND, ... 1411.

RUPRECHT of the Rhine was a good and able man, but there was still a party who made the existence of Wenzel an excuse for obeying nobody, and the new King was not strong enough to force them to obey him. He tried to interfere in the affairs of Italy, which was in a state of great disorder, but he was defeated at Brescia, where the Duke of Austria was made prisoner, and this battle was the last the Germans fought on the other side of the Alps for at least fifty years, during which time the great free towns were nearly all seized by tyrant citizens who took the chief power.

In Germany Ruprecht was more respected, and

put down the injustice of the Markgraf of Baden, who made every one who went through his lands pay a heavy toll. Ruprecht married his eldest son, Ludwig, to Blanche, daughter of Henry IV. of England, but she died at the end of the first year.

On Ruprecht's death in 1410, the Electors went back to the house of Luxemburg, but they were not agreed, half of them taking Jobst of Luxemburg, Markgraf of Moravia, son of a younger son of the blind John of Bohemia, and the other half, his cousin Siegmund, King of Hungary, and Elector of Brandenburg. Jobst was crowned, but died the next year, 1411, and at the diet ensuing, Siegmund, as Elector, voted for himself, saying that there was no one whose good qualities he knew so well as his own. The others agreed to accept him, and he was crowned at Aachen.

He was a clever man, with good intentions, but vain and flighty, and with the restless spirit of all the Luxemburg family. He was anxious to bring the Great Schism to an end, for it was now worse than ever, an attempt at a council having been held which had deposed both Popes and elected another, but as neither would obey it, there were three Popes, just as there had been, during Jobst's

Hus at Constance

life, three Kings of Germany at the same time. The need was the more felt that the teaching of the English John Wickliffe had been brought to Bohemia by the followers of Queen Anne, and had found favor at the University of Prague with two Bohemian scholars, Johann Huss, professor of philosophy, and Jerome Faulfisch, a master of arts. Wenzel had encouraged them, and the more Catholic professors had all gone off in a body to Leipsig. Hussite preaching had spread through Bohemia, and the Czechs were strongly crying out against the Pope's claim to be universal Bishop, and against the denying the Cup in the Holy Communion to the laity, as well as many of the horrid corruptions that had grown up in the Church. One of the worst of these was, that whereas the Popes had ventured to declare that whoever went on a crusade or on a pilgrimage to Rome would be freed from a certain number of years of purifying fire, which was called Purgatory; it had lately been said that indulgences, remitting part of the penance, might be had for money, which was supposed to go in alms, but was generally spent on the needs of the Pope and his Cardinals.

Siegmund was bent on holding a Council to set all these abuses to rights. He went to France and

Italy, and at last in November, 1414, he brought together one of the three Popes, John XXIII., 3 Patriarchs, 33 Cardinals, 47 Archbishops, 145 Bishops, 224 Abbots, 1800 Priests, and 750 doctors of theology, at Constance. They were followed by a strange crew of all sorts of people, friars, knights, squires, merchants, pedlars, mountebanks, jugglers, beggars, so that all around the city was like an enormous fair. The clergy of each nation were to form different chambers, Italian, German, English, French, and Spanish. It was said of them, "The Germans are imperious and patient, the French boastful and vain, the En-

SIEGMUND.

glish ready and wise, the Italians subtle and intriguing." Siegmund made a speech to open the Council, but he was wrong in his grammar, and when one of the Cardinals corrected him, he said, "I am King of the Romans, and lord of the Latin grammar." The first decision was that a Council of the Church is supreme to the Pope. Then Siegmund told the Council of the promises of the two absent Popes to resign, and John XXIII., finding that horrible stories were coming out against him, made oath that he would do the same, but instead of doing so, he persuaded Friedrich, Duke of Austria, to help him run away to Schaffhausen. However, it was decided that this was the same as an abdication, and Friedrich was severely punished, and forced to give him up to be imprisoned for life.

Then the Council began to consider of doctrine. Siegmund had given a safe-conduct to Johann Huss, to come to and go from Constance, but fearing it would not be respected, Huss tried to escape in a wagon of hay, but he was found and brought back again. Wickliffe's writings were read, and the errors in them condemned, and then John Huss was brought before the Council and forbidden to continue this teaching on pain of death. He would not promise silence, so he was condemned to be burnt, and when he appealed to the King's safe-conduct, Siegmund said that no faith was to be kept with a heretic, and Huss was burnt at a stake outside the town.

The next thing Siegmund did was to go all the way to Perpignan on the Pyrennees to force one of the anti-Popes to resign, and though he failed to do this, he persuaded the Spanish kings to withdraw their support, and promise to own any Pope whom the Council might elect. He gained the same promise from the French by going to Paris, and he then visited England, spent St. George's day at Windsor with Henry V., and was made a Knight of the Garter, and persuaded no less than 400 Englishmen to go to the Council at Constance.

Not much had been done there except the burning of Jerome of Prague; but when the King returned, and Cardinal Beaufort arrived, the Germans, who had tried hard to get the worst abuses reformed before a new Pope was chosen, gave way, and Martin IV. was elected. He hushed up matters by giving to each nation for a time what they most craved for, but staved off any real reformation.

But Huss's death had caused a terrible uproar

in Bohemia, headed by a noble called John Ziska. He marched through Prague, storming the council chamber, and murdering the clergy. King Wenzel was dreadfully excited at the sounds, and one of his servants saying that he had known for three days that there would be an outbreak, he jumped up, caught the man by the hair, and would have killed him; but being withheld by bystanders, fell into a fit and died in 1419. Ziska, with a banner bearing the Chalice, marched through Bohemia, at the head of an army of all ranks, sexes, and ages, committing horrid ravages, though they called themselves God's people. When a battle was fought, he bade the women take off their veils and mantles and throw them on the ground to entangle the feet of the horses of their enemies. Though he soon lost his sight, he was a great captain, using a terrible iron mace which beat down all before him, and he defeated both Siegmund and the Duke of Austria.

He died in the Plague in 1424, but Procop Holy was almost equally successful, and when, in 1431, the council of Basle met to confirm the decrees of Constance, peace was made with the Hussites, or Calixtines, as they termed themselves in honor of the chalice, and they were allowed to have the

Holy Eucharist in both kinds, freedom of preaching, and to keep the property of which they had robbed the priests.

After this, Siegmund was owned as King of Bohemia, and with his second queen, a wicked woman named Barbara Cilly, was crowned at Prague. They had only one daughter named Elizabeth, and Siegmund had given the electoral county of Brandenburg to Friedrich of Hohenzollern, Burgraf of Nuremburg. The kingdoms of Bohemia, Hungary, and the Empire he wished to leave to his daughter's husband, Albrecht, Duke of Austria, but Barbara was scheming to keep them herself, and marry Ladislaf, King of Poland, though he was twenty-three and she sixty, and so she pretended to be a great friend of the Hussites, so as to get their support, though she really believed in nothing.

Siegmund thought his last illness was owing to poison she had given him and ordered her to be arrested. He called the barons of Hungary and Bohemia to his death-bed, and named his son-in-law, Albrecht of Hapsburg, Duke of Austria, as his successor in these kingdoms. He died in Moravia, in his seventieth year, on the 9th of **September, 1438.**

CHAPTER XXIV.

ALBRECHT II., ... 1438–1440.
FRIEDRICH III., ... 1440–1482.

ALBRECHT of Austria had to fight with the Calixtines for the crown of Bohemia, but was accepted at last, and he was also chosen King of Hungary and King of the Romans. He was a good and able man, and as King of Hungary found himself bound to keep back the terrible Othman Turks, who had become the chief Mahometan power. They had crossed the Dardanelles, made their capital at Adrianople, and were threatening Constantinople on the one hand, and Hungary on the other.

Albrecht marched against them, and encamped on the Danube, but he had not men enough to prevent the fall of the Servian city of Semendria, and when he succeeded in collecting an army, the unwholesome marshes in which he was encamped brought on illness which forced him to turn back. He was so ill that his physician begged him to stop at Buda, but he declared that he should be well if he could only see Vienna and his wife again, and was carried forward in a litter to a little village near Gran, where he died at forty-two years old, having only reigned two years. He left two little daughters, and a son who was born after his death, and christened Ladislas or Lassla.

ALBRECHT II.

The Hungarians wanted a man to defend them, and offered their crown to King Ladislas of Poland, but when he came to be crowned, the holy crown of St. Stephen of Hungary could nowhere be found, till Elizabeth with her little son appeared at Weissenberg, and produced the crown, which had been hidden in his cradle. He was crowned with it and knighted at twelve weeks old, but the disputed succession was a miserable thing for all Europe, when Hungary ought to have been the bulwark of Christendom against the Turks. However, the King of Poland was chosen for the present by the great body of Hungarians, and Elizabeth retired into Styria, where she soon died.

The Electors had in the meantime met, and had given the crown to the eldest member of the House of Hapsburg, Friedrich, Duke of Styria, first cousin to Albrecht, a dull indolent man, but very avaricious and grasping. Everything he had was marked with the letters A E I O U, which puzzled every one all his life, but after his death a key was found in his own handwriting.

Latin — Austriæ est Imperare orbi universe.
German — Alles erdreich ist Oesterreich untherthan.

Or, as we may render it in English —

Austria's Empire is over [the] universe.

or

All earth is Oesterrich's underling.

Indeed he thought much of astrology and magic, and cared more for these than for the affairs of the Empire, except that he grasped all the money that came into his possession. He was not Duke of all Austria, which was divided between him and his brother Albrecht, and he had neither Hungary nor Bohemia, but he was the last Emperor who was crowned at Rome, in 1452, and he then made the Austrian title, Erzherzog, or Archduke.

FRIEDRICH III.

His wife was Eleanor of Portugal, a beautiful lady who met him at Siena, and was married to him at Rome by the Pope himself, after which he knighted his young cousin, Lassla, king by right of Bohemia and Hungary. There were prodigious feastings, with tables for 30,000 guests, and the fountains running with wine, but Friedrich was so little thought of in Italy that practical jokes were played on him. As he rode into Viterbo under a canopy of cloth of gold, some young men let down hooks from the balconies above and pulled that up, after which they proceeded to fish for his hat which had a valuable jewel in it, but this was more than Friedrich could bear, he seized a staff, and charged the uncivil crowd. The ringleaders were sent to prison, but released at his request.

Young Lassla died in 1457, and Bohemia chose for king, George Podiebrad, a Hussite noble, while the Hungarians elected Matthias Corvinus, son of John Huniades, a nobleman who had bravely defended them against the Turks — who, in 1453, had taken Constantinople, and were more dangerous than ever. Friedrich was greatly disliked even in Austria, and was actually besieged in the fortress of Vienna with his wife and child by the populace, till he was delivered by George Podiebrad, whom he rewarded by owning him as King of Bohemia.

His brother Albrecht died in 1463, and he then gained the rest of Austria, except the Tyrol, which belonged to his cousin Siegmund, as did also Elsass. Siegmund being an extravagant, needy prince, mortgaged Elsass to the great Duke of Burgundy,

Charles the Bold, who had inherited Flanders, Holland, and all the lands at the mouths of the Rhine, Maes, &c., which were partly fiefs of Germany and partly of France; Charles was like the king of all this, the richest country in Europe, and as he had only one child, Mary of Burgundy, he proposed to marry her to Maximilian, the only son of Friedrich, on being himself elected King of the Romans. Thus, after his death, Maximilian and Mary would reign together, and large hereditary possessions would be added to Austria. Friedrich and his son met Charles at Trier. Maximilian, whose name had been invented by his father as a compound of Maximus and Æmilianus, was a splendid young man of eighteen, with long, fair hair, a great contrast to his dull, heavy father, who was lame from a disease in his foot, brought on by a habit of always kicking doors open.

There were eight weeks of feasting and tilting at Charles's expense, and preparations were made for Charles's coronation as King of the Romans, when five out of the seven Electors, angry that their consent should have been taken for granted, and for different reasons disliking Charles, persuaded the Emperor out of the scheme, and in the middle of the night Friedrich stole down to the river Moselle, took boat, and had reached Köln before his flight was discovered. He had left all his debts unpaid, and no farewells for his host.

The Duchy of Lorraine had been seized on by Charles, and the rightful heir, Réne of Vandémont, was fighting hard for it, supported secretly by Louis XI. of France, the great foe of Burgundy. And Siegmund had hopes of getting back Elsass without paying the sum it was pawned for, since Charles's governor, Peter von Hagenbach, was harsh and cruel, and hated by the people, who jointly with a band of Swiss, rose against him, and put him to death at Breisach. There broke out a great war between Burgundy on the one hand, and Lorraine, Elsass, and Switzerland on the other. The Swiss overthrew the knights in two great battles at Granson and Muret, and finally, while Charles was besieging Nancy, the capital of Lorraine, they came down on his camp in the dawn of the Twelfth day morning of the year 1477, broke up his fine army, and left him lying dead in a frozen pool.

His young daughter did not inherit Burgundy, but was heiress to the many counties of Holland and the Netherlands. She was beset by Louis XI., who wanted to marry her to his son, and her own subjects in the great Flemish towns were turbulent and factious, and put her father's trusty old councillors to death for a supposed intrigue with France. In her distress she sent Maximilian a ring, and he hastened to her aid, and married her at once. For three years they were most happy together, then in 1482 she was killed by a fall from her horse, leaving two little children, Philip and Margarethe.

CHAPTER XXV.

FRIEDRICH III., ... 1482–1493.

FRIEDRICH III. was in trouble at home while his son was in the Low Countries. The Pope would not own George Podiebrad as King of Bohemia, because he was a Calixtine, and a crusade against him was preached in Germany and Austria. In much anger, George invaded Austria, and brought the Emperor to such distress that he promised to support Matthias Corvinus, who had been elected by the Bohemian Catholics, if he would defend Austria.

However he then grew alarmed at the notion of the two kingdoms being joined under so great a leader as Matthias, and when George proposed to the Bohemians, Ladislas, the son of the King of Poland, and of Elizabeth, the daughter of Albrecht

II., he gave the measure his support, and Ladislas, claimed the crown on George's death.

Matthias was very angry at Friedrich's treachery. He defeated the Polish army which was supporting Ladislas, and also gained a great victory over the Turks, and took the fortress of Saltzbach on the Danube, which was a great protection against the Othman power. Then he invaded Austria, where the Emperor made no resistance, but fled from Vienna and went wandering about from city to city and convent to convent, seeking help which he could not find.

Nor could his son give him any aid, for the States of Flanders and Holland would not let Maximilian have the charge of them for his little son after his wife's death but concluded a treaty with Louis XI. of France, and sent the infant Margarethe to be brought up at Paris for a wife for the Dauphin Charles. However, at a diet at Frankfort, the Electors chose Maximilian King of the Romans, and soon after, Anne, the heiress of Brittany, who was sorely pressed by the French on one hand, and her own people on the other, sent to beg him to come and marry her, and save her from her enemies. He set out with a troop of Germans, but he had to pass through the city of Bruges, and there the burghers were so angry at his bringing Germans into Flanders, that when he came into the town with only his own attendants, they rose upon him, and drove him into an apothecary's shop, whence he was taken to the castle and kept a prisoner for ten months, till the German princes collected an army and forced the Flemings to make terms, and to set him free. He behaved through the whole time with the greatest patience and good humor, and after giving thanks for his freedom in the Church at Bruges, turned to the citizens and said, "We are now at peace." By that time Anne of Brittany had become the wife of that very Charles of France who had been betrothed to Maximilian's daughter Margarethe, and she was sent back to Brussels, father and daughter being thus both disappointed.

Maximilian was a fine tall graceful man, who had studied all that was then known of language, art, and science, and was brave to rashness. He went into a den with some lions, and when the door closed on him, and they turned on him, he defended himself with a shovel till help came. He climbed to the topmost pinnacle of the spire of Ulm Cathedral, and stood there with half one foot overhanging. He was a most fearless chamois hunter, and had been in many terrible dangers from winds and avalanches in the Tyrolean mountains. Once he slipped down a precipice called the Martinswand, and was caught by a small ledge of rock with a cleft behind it, whence there was no way up or down. The whole population came out and saw him, but could do nothing to help him, or hinder him from being starved. He threw down a stone with a paper fastened to it, begging that Mass might be celebrated below, and a shot fired to let him know the moment of the consecration. At night, however, he suddenly appeared among his friends, saying that a shepherd boy had come and led him through a passage in the cleft through the mountain, and brought him back in safety. This shepherd was never seen again, and was believed by the Tyrolese to have been an angel. A little church built by Maximilian still stands on the top of the rock.

For his daring courage he was called the Last of the Knights, and he made many experiments on the management of fire-arms, which were just coming into general use. In these he ran great risks and had hairbreadth escapes. Once the long-pointed toe of his boot was caught and torn off by the wheel of a machine for turning stone cannon-balls, and another time he was just in time to de-

Maximilian and Albert Durer.

tect his fool putting a match to the mouth of a cannon before which he was standing. He made, however, many improvements in the artillery of the time, he greatly encouraged printing, and especially favored the great Nuremburg painter, Albrecht Durer. He even wrote in great part two curious books called "Theurdank" and "The White King," in which he describes his whole life and adventures in a sort of allegory, in both bringing in his marriage with Marie of Burgundy, for whom he never ceased to mourn all his life.

Meantime the misrule and lawlessness of Germany were unbearable. A robber knight called Kunz of Kauffingen, in 1455, actually scaled the Castle of Altenberg, belonging to the Elector Friedrich the Mild of Saxony, in the middle of the night, and stole his two little sons, Ernst and Albrecht. Ernst was hidden by some of the band in a cave, but Kunz himself, carrying Albrecht before him on his horse, halted in a forest at daybreak, and dismounted to refresh the child with some wild strawberries. A charcoal-burner came up at the moment, and Albrecht shrieked out to him for help, when he laid about him so gallantly with his long pole, that he detained Kunz till at his whistle other woodmen came up, the boy was rescued, and the robber taken. His gang then gave up the other child to his parents, and Kunz was beheaded at Freiburg a week later.

The princes and cities began to exert themselves to prevent such outrages, the Swabian League especially, feud letters were strictly forbidden, and the castles on the mountains where the nobles had held out against all law and order were stormed, and the nobles reduced to submission, or else put to death. In all this the Emperor took little part, being chiefly taken up with astrology and alchemy, and with hoarding treasure, and indeed he behaved shamefully in withholding the ransoms of his own Austrian nobles who had been made prisoners by the Turks.

When Siegmund of Hapsburg died he left Tyrol to Albrecht, Duke of Bavaria, who had married Friedrich's daughter, Kunigunde. He also seized the great imperial city of Regensburg, but with the aid of the Swabian League he was reduced to make peace by the mediation of Maximilian. The high qualities of the King of the Romans had led Matthias Corvinus to be willing to make him his heir, but the Magyars chose instead Ladislas of Poland, who was already King of Bohemia.

Friedrich was seventy-eight years old when he

had his diseased leg cut off. He took it in his hand, saying, "There! a sound boor is better than a sick Kaisar." He seemed to be going on well, but he ate too plentifully of melons, and died on the 19th of August, 1493, having reigned fifty-three years, a reign longer than that of any Emperor except Augustus.

CHAPTER XXVI.

MAXIMILIAN,............1493-1519.

KAISAR Max, as every one called him, though he never was crowned as Emperor, began by gallantly driving back the Turks, who had advanced as far as Laybach, so that he was hailed at Innspruck, his favorite city, as a deliverer.

He then married Bianca Maria, the sister of Giovanni Galeazzo, Duke of Milan, because he wished to have a footing in Italy, but he never loved her like the wife of his youth, and she seems to have been a dull, heavy woman, who grew inordinately fat from eating snails. The affairs of Italy were the great concern, for Bianca's uncle, Ludovico Sforza, after having brought about an invasion of Italy by Charles VIII. of France, was ready to do anything to get rid of him. Maximilian joined the league against him, and for many years there was a continual struggle in Italy between Germans, French, and Spaniards, the Italians themselves sometimes taking part with one, sometimes with

MAXIMILIAN.

the other, and only wishing to get rid of them all alike as foreigners. The Pope, Alexander VI., was one of the worst of men, and had brought the Church into such a state, that all good men felt that there was no cure but calling a General Council. Philip, the son of Maximilian and Marie of Burgundy, had been married to Juana, the daughter of Ferdinand, King of Aragon, and Isabel, Queen of Castille. He died in 1504, leaving two sons, Charles and Ferdinand, and five daughters. His wife became insane with grief, and the children were brought up by Margarethe, his sister, who ruled their inheritance of the Low Countries with great wisdom and skill. She and her father wrote very amusing letters to one another, which are still preserved.

She was sent to manage a treaty which Maximilian made with Louis XII. of France against the republic of Venice, and met the French minister, the Cardinal of Amboise, at Cambrai, where she wrote to her father he and she were nearly ready to pull each other's hair, but at last they agreed to attack the Venetians, who had beaten the Germans and laughed at the Kaisar, calling him Maximilian the moneyless. Both he and Louis XII. crossed the Alps, but the German nobles had little mind for the war, and the only troops he could trust were the landsknechts, foot soldiers of low birth, who carried heavy pikes, formed troops under captains of their own, and hired themselves out to fight. At the siege of Padua, Maximilian asked the French knights to storm the place together with the landsknechts, but they made answer that they would not do so unless the German knights likewise joined in the assault. Maximilian thought this fair, but the German nobility made answer that they would only fight on horseback, and that it was beneath them to dismount and scramble through ditches and walls. The Kaisar was so much ashamed of them that he set out at night with only five men, rode forty miles without stopping, sent orders to break up the camp, and retired to Austria.

He was always making great schemes, and breaking down suddenly in them for want of money, or of the support of his princes, and thus, though he was the cleverest sovereign on the throne, and with the highest ideas and noblest notions, he was little trusted or respected, and he did very strange things. Julius II. drew him and Henry VIII. into what he called the Holy League, for driving the French out of Italy, and when Henry attacked them at home, and laid siege to Terouenne, Maximilian went and served in his army as a private knight for 100 crowns a-day.

And when Julius II. died, Maximilian actually tried to be elected Pope, thinking that thus he could best call a council and reform the Church, but he was not attended to, and Pope Leo X. was chosen. All this made foreign nations laugh at him and think him untrustworthy, but his failures were chiefly owing to the disobedience and want of public spirit of the German princes. He once said the King of France reigned over asses, for they would bear any burthen he pleased; the King of Spain was a king of men, who only submitted in reason; the King of England was a king of angels, who did him willing, faithful service; but the Kaisar reigned over kings who only obeyed him when they chose.

And that was seldom. The Germans were in a bad state, rude and boorish, too poor and too proud to seek improvements, drunkards and great sticklers for rank. The free cities were much better in some ways, but two of them actually went to war because a maiden of one refused to dance with a young burgher of the other. Maximilian suffered in authority by the loss of Bohemia, and Switzerland entirely broke off from the Empire, but he did

Luther and his Thesis.

much toward setting things in a better state for the future, by dividing the Empire into circles, Bavaria, Swabia, Franconia, Austria, Burgundy, Upper and Lower Saxony, and the Upper and Lower Rhine. A governor was placed over each circle, whose duty it was to carry out the decisions of the diet and to keep order. Austria was kept in excellent order, and there was a court set up to hear appeals from the country. It was called the Aulic Council, from Aula, a hall, and became very important. But do what he would, the Germans had not public spirit enough to join their Kaisar in attacking the Turks, who grew more dangerous every year. Maximilian vainly appealed to them. A very large meteoric stone which came down near Encisheim was held to be a thunderbolt, and Maximilian had it hung up in the Church, to show what might be looked for from the wrath of Heaven, but all in vain. No one heeded his warnings.

The wisest man in Germany was the good Elector of Saxony, Friedrich, son of the Albrecht who had been stolen. He had founded a university at Wittenberg, and here one of the professors was Martin Luther, the son of a woodcutter of Thuringia, who had struggled into getting educated at the University of Erfurt, and had become a monk. He had been much troubled in mind by the sense of sin, until a good old monk taught him to think most of the Merits of his Saviour. He read the Bible with all his might, and became a great preacher, as well as a doctor of theology at Wittenberg. A friar named John Tetzel came to the neighborhood selling indulgences, and saying such shocking things to recommend them, that Luther's spirit was stirred, and on the 31st of October, 1517, he nailed to the door at Wittenberg a paper called a thesis, in which he challenged the whole system on which the sale of indulgences was founded. The thesis was printed, and spread all over Germany, so that there was a vehement controversy, in which Maximilian took some interest, but he was much taken up with trying to secure the Empire to his grandson Charles, and likewise with the endeavor to raise Germany against the Turks. For this purpose he held a diet at Augsburg, but a knight named Ulrich of Hutten sent round a paper calling the Pope a worse foe to Christendom than the Sultan, and the princes disputed and did nothing. The Kaisar went away grieved, and soon after fell ill of a fever, and died at Well in Austria in his fifty-ninth year, in 1519. A chest he had always carried about with him for the last four years turned out to be his coffin, and he was buried by his own desire at Neustadt, though he had built himself a most beautiful monument at Innspruck.

CHAPTER XXVII.

CHARLES V., ... 1519–1529.

ON the death of Maximilian, the Empire was coveted by three kings, Henry VIII. of England, Francis I. of France, and Charles* of Spain. Henry, however, on enquiry, found that he was better off in England than he would have been with the addition of the stormy Empire, and gave up all thoughts of offering himself, but Francis declared that he and Charles were both suitors for the same lady, and sent wagon-loads of treasure to decide her choice.

The Electors, however, wished to choose the good Frederick the Wise of Saxony, and would have done so but that he declared that the Emperor ought to have much larger lands of his own

---

* In Germany Karl, in Spain Carlos, but he is generally known by his Flemish name Charles.

than his half of Saxony, in order to be able to protect the country from the Turks, and he also thought himself too old for such a charge. He,

CHARLES V.

therefore, led them to choose the late Kaisar's grandson, Charles of Hapsburg, Archduke of Austria, and lord of all the little fiefs that made up the

Low Countries, as well as King of all Spain, Naples, and Sicily, though his mother, the poor crazy Juana, was still alive, watching her husband's coffin, in hopes that he would wake again.

Charles had been born at Ghent with the century, and was only nineteen. His aunt Margarethe had educated him at Brussels, and he was more of a Fleming than anything else. He was the exact contrary of his brilliant grandfather, grave, silent, thoughtful, very slow in making up his mind, but never changing his purpose when he had once decided. He was long in growing up, and had a sensitive nervous timidity about him, which he only kept under by very strong self-control. He was a religious man, and anxious for the good of the Church, and he set before him from the first two great works as the duty of the head of the Holy Roman Empire — namely, to hold a general council for the purifying of the Church, and to have a crusade to drive back the Turks; but in both these he was hindered all through his reign by the jealously of Francis I.

Luther wrote to him on the state of the Church in strong and bitter words, and at the same time Pope Leo X. put forth a bull denouncing Luther's teaching, and commanding that if he did not recant within sixty days he should be sent to Rome and dealt with as a heretic. This bull was burnt by Luther and his scholars in the market-place at Wittenberg, all his friends refused to publish it, and he appealed from it to a General Council of the Church.

Charles called together a Diet to meet at Wurms, on the 6th of January, 1521, and invited Luther thither with a safe-conduct. It was feared that this might be no more heeded than the safe-conduct of Siegmund to Huss, but Luther declared he would go "though there should be as many devils at Wurms as there were tiles on the roofs," and he came into the city in a wagon chanting Psalms.

The Diet was the largest that had ever met in Germany, for Luther's friends mustered there to protect him, and an old captain of landsknechts, George of Freundsburg, came and shook him by the hand, saying, "Little monk, thou art on a march, and charge such as we captains never saw in our bloodiest battle, but if thy cause be just, On in God's name, He will not forsake thee." Luther was asked whether he had written the books that were before the Diet. He said yes, and began to defend himself in Latin. Charles deemed him rough and coarse, and said, "This is not the man to make me a heretic." The Emperor thought a Diet was not the place for discussing religious matters, and so would only have him asked by the Chancellor whether he would recant, or run the risks of the law against heretics. Luther looked around, and said, "Here I am. I can no otherwise. God help me. Amen."

The clergy held other arguments with him, but he had gone on to dispute many doctrines besides that of the power of the Pope to pardon sin, and it was plain there could be no agreement. Charles would not let his safe-conduct be violated, but Luther's friends, not trusting to this, sent him away secretly by night, and fearing he might be arrested at Wittenberg, the Elector of Saxony caused him to be waylaid on the road by men who passed for robbers. They disguised him as a Junker, as squires were called, and carried him off to the Tower of Wartburg, where he spent his time in translating the Bible into German.

Charles at this Diet divided his lands of Austria with his younger brother Ferdinand, who married Anne, the daughter of Ladislaf, King of Hungary and Bohemia. Ferdinand was a man whom every one liked, and was a most faithful brother to Charles, who left him to govern in Germany when

Luther at Wartburg.

he himself was obliged to return to Spain, because his old tutor, Adrian of Utrecht, whom he had left to govern there, had been chosen Pope. Adrian was a good man, and Charles hoped by his help to reform the Church, but he was too good for the wicked court of Rome, and was soon poisoned. A Pope was elected, named Clement VII., whose great desire was to prevent any council that could lessen the gains of the Pope and Cardinals.

Francis I. had begun a war almost immediately on Charles's election, on four different quarrels, namely, the kingdom of Naples, the dukedom of Milan, and the French fiefs of the Low Countries, all which Francis said belonged to him, and the kingdom of Navarre, which was a Spanish quarrel. Charles said that he praised God that he did not begin the war, and that when they left off, one or other of them would be much poorer than when they began.

And indeed, in the Spaniards Charles had the very best soldiers then in the world, and could do almost anything with them, so that he at once drove the French out of Milan. His chief general was the Marquis of Pescara, a Neapolitan noble, and on a quarrel with his master, the chief nobleman in France, the Constable of Bourbon deserted to him. The King invaded Italy and beseiged Pavia, but Pescara and Bourbon marched against him, routed his army, made him prisoner, and sent him to Charles at Madrid. Charles would have no rejoicings, as he said that a war between Christian kings was only a matter for sorrow. He would only release Francis on condition of his giving up all claims to the Sicilies and Milan, and also the duchy of Burgundy, which had gone back to the crown on the death of Charles the Bold. Francis raged at first and said he would rather give up his crown, but soon he pined himself ill, and then made an oath, with no subject of Charles to hear him, that he was under constraint, and should not hold himself bound by his promises. Then he engaged to do all Charles had demanded, and was taken to the frontier and set free, giving his two little sons as hostages.

But he would not keep his word nor give up the duchy of Burgundy, and made a league with Clement VII., who wanted to prevent the Emperor from forcing him to call a council. He suffered, however, for this league, for there were a number of wild landsknechts in the north of Italy, with the Constable of Bourbon and George of Freundsberg, and they took it into their heads to march to Rome and plunder it, meaning to go on to Naples, and make Bourbon king. The Pope had no troops able to make much defence, though Bourbon was shot dead as he was about to enter. The lawless soldiers spread all over the city, and the Pope shut himself up in the Castle of St. Angelo. There was horrible cruelty, plunder, and sacrilege for many days, before the soldiers, fairly worn out with their excesses, could be got out of Rome by Lannoy, Charles's Flemish governor of Naples. The French army in the north of Italy caught the plague that had begun among the landsknechts at Rome, and nearly all perished, and Francis was obliged again to make peace. His mother and Charles's aunt Margarethe met at Cambria and settled the terms. It was called the Ladies' Peace, and was signed in 1529.

CHAPTER XXVIII.

CHARLES V............1530-1535.

AFTER the Ladies' Peace was signed, Charles V. met Clement VIII. at Bologna, and was crowned King of Italy and Roman Emperor. He urged Clement so strongly to hold a council that there was no withstanding him. The Pope promised to send out letters, and Charles went to hold a diet at Augsburg, to take measures for driving back the Turks, and setting Europe at peace from without as well as within.

During the nine years since the Diet of Wurms, the opinions of Luther had made great progress. Luther had, after about eighteen months, come back from Wartburg, because Carlstadt, one of his pupils, was doing such wild things at Wittenberg, that it was needful to interfere. Luther had, however, come to think convents and monastic vows were harmful, and those monks and nuns who accepted his teaching left their convents, and many priests married. There was no vow to hinder priests from wedlock, but monks and nuns had promised not to marry. However, Luther thought them not binding, and himself married Katherine Bora, one of five nuns who had been carried out of their convent in empty beer barrels.

When all these changes were happening, the peasants, who had been horribly ill-used for ages, made a great rising in Swabia, Franconia, Elsass, and Thuringia. Their chief leader was one Thomas Münzer, who declared that all men's goods ought to be in common, and led about a host of miners, laborers, and woodmen, who perpetrated the most horrid cruelties on the unfortunate nobles and ladies who fell into their hands, and forced some of the knights to march in their ranks, while they wandered about, sacking every castle and convent whose walls were not strong enough to keep them out. Troops were raised by Philip, Landgraf of Hesse, Heinrich, Duke of Brunswick, and Johann, brother of the Elector of Saxony, and met the peasants at Frankenhausen. Münzer pointed to a rainbow in the sky, and told his poor deluded followers that it was the pledge of victory, but they were trodden down by the well-armed knights and slaughtered like sheep. Münzer himself was found hidden in a hayloft and executed. One prisoner, when asked how he had fared, said, "Ah, sir! the rule of the peasants is ten times worse than the rule of a knight." Every one was hot against these unhappy peasants, except the good Elector Friedrich, who said if they were brutal savages it was the fault of the princes who had left them to become so, and whose heart was broken by the evils around him. He died soon after, saying he knew not where to find faith or truth on earth, and was succeeded by his brother Johann.

A diet had been held by the Archduke Ferdinand at Speier, in the hope of opening the eyes of the Germans to the need of supporting his brother-in-law, Ludwig, King of Hungary, against the Turks, but they would attend to nothing but the disputes between Luther and the Church, and he could get no aid against the common enemy, while they decided that each prince might have whatever form of doctrine he chose in his lands, and thereupon the Elector of Saxony, the Landgraf of Hesse, and some others, had all the churches given over to the Lutherans, and seized the abbeys and the lands of the bishoprics. Albrecht of Brandenburg, Grand Master of the Teutonic Order of Knights, followed their example, helped himself to the lands of the Order in Prussia, and obtained investiture of them from the King of Poland.

Thus left unaided, Ludwig of Hungary and Bohemia was defeated and killed by the Turks in the terrible battle of Mohatz, in 1527. Ferdinand was at once chosen King of Bohemia, but a Transylvanian, named Johann Zapoyla, was chosen King of Hungary, and called in the Sultan Solyman to support him. They even laid siege to Vienna, but Ferdinand beat them off, drove the Turks beyond the Danube, and was crowned King of Hungary. Bohemia and Hungary have ever since had kings of the House of Austria.

Ferdinand being now stronger, held another diet at Speier, in 1529, where the Catholics were in the larger numbers, and ordained that, till the council should be held, there should be no more changes in religion, and that Mass should be said in the churches. The Lutherans made a protest against this edict, and they were therefore called Protestants. The name gradually spread to all who broke from the Roman Catholic Church, but it properly meant those who protested against the edict of Speier.

It was high time that Charles should be at home, and he came immediately after his coronation in 1530, and summoned a great diet at Augsburg. The Protestants prepared for it by drawing up a great confession of their faith. It was chiefly the work of Philip Melancthon, a very good and learned man, a great friend of Luther, and it has ever since been looked upon as the great rule of faith of the Lutherans.

The Protestants wanted to read the confession in the great hall of the council, but this was not permitted, and it was read in a chapel that would only hold 200 persons, but as the windows were open, every one who chose could hear it. Charles, not knowing German well, wished it to be read in Latin, but Johann of Saxony said that on German soil it must be read in the mother tongue. Charles listened courteously, and accepted a copy both in Latin and German, but gave no opinion, since all was to be put off to the council, and in the meantime the Latin service and old rites were to go on. Philip of Hesse and Johann of Saxony on this went off from the diet, and with five more princes

Charles V and Fugger.

and twelve towns formed, at the city of Schmalkalde, a league for the defence of their doctrine.

In the meantime the rest of the diet elected the Emperor's brother, Ferdinand, King of the Romans, and Charles strove with all his might to array his forces for an attack on the Turks, but the league refused to stir unless he permitted the Protestants to have their own way.

The need was so great that, at Nuremburg, Charles made peace, consenting that things should remain as they were till the council, and he thus succeeded in getting the Germans together to the number of 120,000, upon which the Sultan retreated and left Hungary in peace.

Charles now determined to attack the Turks and their allies the Moors in their settlement on the coast of Africa, where there were several seaports, such as Tunis and Algiers, which were perfect nests of pirates. These Moorish ships continually tormented the coasts of Spain and Italy, carrying off the inhabitants, and forcing them to the miserable life of slaves, rowing their galleys, until some ransom should arrive. To put an end to these robberies, Charles mustered all his Aragonese ships as well as the German soldiers, and with the aid of the Genoese and the Knights of St. John, he most gallantly captured Tunis, and set free no less than 22,000 Christian slaves, who were shut up in dungeons, toiling in gardens, or at the fortifications, or laboring at the oar.

He had been obliged to borrow very heavily of the great merchant, Fugger of Augsburg, to fit out this expedition. The next time he came to Augsburg, Fugger begged for the honor of entertaining him. A fire was burning on the hearth full of sweet odors from precious spices and woods. The Emperor said it was the most costly fire he had ever seen. "It shall be more costly still," said the merchant, and into it he threw all the bonds for the sum due to him from Charles.

CHAPTER XXIX.

CHARLES V., ... 1535.

IT was not till Clement VII. and Francis I. were both dead that Charles V., after fifteen years' waiting, was able to have the Council of the Western Church really summoned. Clement was always putting it off, and Francis took advantage of every disaster that befell Charles to harass him. In an expedition which Charles made to Algiers, his fleet was shattered by a tempest, and Francis immediately began a fresh war with him; and when Charles had to ask leave to travel through France, when he wanted to go from Spain to Flanders, Francis feasted him splendidly, but tormented him to give the duchy of Milan to the Dauphin Henry.

When, however, these two were dead, Pope Paul II. called on the Council to meet at Trent in the Tyrol, but in the time that had been lost the Protestants had grown much more hostile. Luther, who had always been loyal to the Kaisar, was dead, and so was Henry VIII. of England, so that it was much more difficult to get together any but Spanish, and Italian, and Austrian clergy, all strong Roman Catholics. They met in 1545, and the first thing they did was to condemn all translations of the Bible that were not the same with the Latin one made by St. Jerome in the fifth century, and this showed the Lutherans, as they said, that there was no chance for them of a fair hearing, so they refused to come. The head of the Schmalkaldic League was now Johann Friedrich, Elector of Saxony, nephew to Friedrich the Wise, and a war began between him and the Emperor. They were on the opposite sides of the river Elbe at Muhldorf. A miller, whose horses the Saxons had seized, showed the Emperor's Spaniards the way across the river, and Johann Friedrich was surprised in his camp. He fought bravely, but was made prisoner, and led to Charles. His kinsman, Moritz, Duke of the other half of Saxony, had married the daughter of Philip, Landgraf of Hesse. Though he was a Lutheran, he held with the Emperor, who promised to make him Elector instead of Johann

Friedrich. Sybilla of Cleves, wife to Johann Friedrich, held out Wittenberg against the Emperor, but Charles made it known that he should behead the Elector unless the city were given up, and she was obliged to yield. When he came into the city he would not let his Spanish subjects disturb Luther in his grave, nor would he stop the Lutheran service, saying his war was, not with religion, but with treason.

The other Protestant princes were forced to surrender, one by one. Moritz of Saxony brought in his father-in-law, Philip of Hesse, on the understanding that he should be safe, without any (*einiges*) imprisonment, but Charles caused him to be shut up in a fortress, and it appeared that the word they had read *einiges* was really *ewiges*, or perpetual. This was viewed as a terrible breach of Charles's word.

He had forced the Protestants to send representatives to the Council, but behold, there was no Council to go to. Paul II. had been drawn by his greedy kindred, the Farnese family, to ask for lands in Italy that Charles would not grant, and then had allied himself with Henry II. of France, begun a war in Italy, and called back his Italians from the Council.

No more could be done, and Charles was bitterly disappointed. He called together a diet at Augsburg to settle what was to be done. The Germans were very angry at the defeat of their princes by his Spanish soldiers, and looked on him more as a foreign conqueror than as their Emperor; and, on the other hand, many of them were so coarse and boorish, and such drunkards, that Charles, and the Flemish, Spanish, and Italian gentlemen despised them. All Charles could do was to cause one Lutheran and two Catholic divines to draw up a code of rules for worship that might be observed in the Interim, till the Council could meet again, but this Interim pleased no one, and was distrusted by everybody.

Charles further offended the Germans by showing that he wanted them to engage to elect his son Philip King of the Romans when Ferdinand should become Emperor, instead of Ferdinand's son, Maximilian. Philip would of course be King of Spain, and he was a thorough Spaniard, grave, cold, and gloomy, while Maximilian was a bright, kindly, gracious German. They would make no such promise, and showed further displeasure when Charles refused to release Philip of Hesse, and on this Moritz of Saxony began plotting against him.

Flight of Charles V

The city of Magdeburg had never accepted the Interim, and Moritz had been sent to reduce it. He turned the army he was commanding against the Kaisar himself, allied himself with Henry II. of France, and joined the discontented Germans just when half of Charles's Spanish troops were in Hungary fighting with the Turks, and the other half in Italy, and he himself was lying ill of the gout at Innspruck, whither he had gone to try to collect the Council once more. Such a sudden dash did Moritz make at Innspruck that the Emperor had to rise from his bed, and be carried in a litter over the mountain passes by torchlight. He released the Elector, Johann Friedrich, who, however, came with him rather than fall into the hands of his kinsman. Moritz would have pursued them, but his troops stopped to plunder Innspruck, and Charles safely reached the fortress of Villach in Carinthia.

The King of the Romans had a conference with Moritz at Passau, and agreed to his conditions — viz., that the Landgraf should be released, and that each German prince might have such worship as he chose in his dominions, on which Moritz promised himself to head a crusade against the Turks. The Kaisar was forced to consent, though very unwillingly, and Albrecht of Brandenburg refused to be included in the treaty, being really nothing but a savage robber, whose cruelties were shocking. Moritz marched against him, and defeated him at Sievenhausen, but was killed in the moment of victory, when only thirty-two years old. Albrecht fled into France, and there soon died, but his family still held the lands of the Teutonic order which he had seized.

Henry II. of France had allied himself with Moritz, called himself the Protector of the Liberties of Germany, and, with this excuse, seized the three Bishoprics of Metz, Toul, and Verdun. Charles in vain tried to retake Metz. He was much broken and aged, and had been deeply grieved by the failure of the Council and the treason of Moritz, whom he had loved like a son. At a diet held at Augsburg, in 1555, a religious peace was agreed to, leaving the princes free to establish what faith they chose, and the next year the Emperor, who had long ago made up his mind to give up his crowns, and spend his age in devotion, collected his people at Brussels, and there gave up his kingdoms of Spain, Naples, and the Low Countries to his son Philip, and Austria to his brother Ferdinand.

He then retired to the Convent of Yusle in Spain,

Charles V in the Cloister St. Just.

where he spent his time in prayers, and in his garden, and in writing letters of advice to his son. One of his great pleasures was studying mechanics and watchmaking, and there is a story that, when he found no two of his clocks would keep quite the same time, he said that it was just the same with men's minds. His two sisters, the widowed Queens of France and Hungary, lived near, and saw him constantly, and he led a tranquil life till his death in 1558.

CHAPTER XXX.

FERDINAND I............ .... 1556–1564.

FERDINAND I. was already well known and much loved and respected in Germany, where he had served his brother faithfully, and yet won the hearts of all the Germans, who knew him to be perfectly faithful to his word; so much so that when a nobleman to whom he had promised some favor acted so as not to deserve it, he still gave it, saying he cared more for his honor, than for the man's dishonor.

The fierce old Pope, Paul IV., who was chosen in 1555, hated all the House of Austria, because he was a Neapolitan, and Spain had conquered his native kingdom, and he would not acknowledge Ferdinand except on condition of his giving up the peace of Augsburg and persecuting the Protestants. But this Ferdinand would not do, for the peace had been chiefly of his own making, and he believed that if the Pope would give up some of the customs of the Church of Rome they might yet be brought

FERDINAND I.

back to it. Indeed he sent into Bohemia the Jesuits, a body of priests who had been formed in Spain, specially to attend to education and to the training of consciences, and they brought over a great many of the old Hussites to the Church.

Though Ferdinand kept out of the old war between Spain and France, while that was still going on there was no chance of calling together again the Council of Trent; but when at last Henry II. of France was thoroughly beaten in the battle of St. Quentin by Philip II. of Spain, both Emperor and Pope were anxious for it, and Bulls were issued inviting all nations thereto, and also the Protestants. The Protestants met at Naumburg in Saxony to receive the message, which was sent to them by Cardinal Commendone. The Elector August, son to Moritz, took the lead, and told the Cardinal that they could not accept the letters because the Pope called them his sons and they did not own him for their father; and they spoke so violently that he answered them thus— "What, mean ye by these bitter words against one who hath undertaken a long journey in the cause of Christian unity?" And then he reproached them for their many divisions and irreverent ways, saying that over the wine-pot and the dice-box people disputed on the mysteries of religion. They were a little subdued by this rebuke, but they ended by declaring that whatever the Council might say, they would hold to the Confession of Augsburg. Only the Elector Palatine, who had taken up the teachings of Calvin, which went even further from the Roman doctrine than did those of Luther, was very loth to sign the Confession.

The Council met at Trent, and Ferdinand tried to get the Bishops to consent to give the Cup to the laity, to let priests be married men, to have parts of the service in the language of the country, to put a stop to selling indulgences, and to have fewer Cardinals, and better rules for electing the Pope. The French wished for these things also, but the Italians were against all change and joined with the Spaniards against them. There was much fierce quarrelling, and at last, though some rules were made, which have kept the Roman Catholic clergy in better order ever since, and prevented indulgences from ever being sold, they would make no other real reform, and destroyed all hope of bringing back the Protestants and Calvinists. Ferdinand said the Council would do no good if it sat for a hundred years, and was very glad to have it broken up. However, in Germany, to please the Emperor, the Pope, for a time, allowed the administration of the Cup and the marriage of the clergy, and Ferdinand strove hard to bring about the other matters he had asked for. He succeeded so far that there is a part of the service still in German instead of Latin in Austria and the Tyrol.

Indeed Ferdinand was a great peacemaker, and a thoroughly good man. His wife, Anne of Hungary, was an excellent woman, and his eldest son, Maximilian, was so much beloved that the Electors heartily chose him as King of the Romans. He was the first to be so chosen, without the coronation of an Emperor by the Pope to make way for him.

Good as were the Imperial family, the Empire was in a sad state; indeed it had been growing backwards rather than forwards in all good things ever since the time of Friedrich Barbarossa. Then the Germans had been quite equal with the English, French, and Italians in all matters of improvement and civilization, but first the Italian wars called off their Emperors, and then there were quarrels about their election, and those who had only small hereditary possessions were not strong enough to keep the princes and nobles in order. The greater princes and the free towns managed to establish some rule, and the Swabian League had destroyed the worst of the lesser independent nobles. Maximilian's arrangement of the circles did some good, but Charles the Fifth's reign had only made things worse, by adding quarrels between Protestant and Roman Catholic to all the rest. He had indeed subdued the German princes by his Spanish troops, but they felt as if a foreigner had conquered them, and hated him. Almost every mountain pass had a robber noble, who tormented travelers, and ground down his vassals by his exactions. The nobles despised learning, and were terrible drunkards and gamesters, so that their diets and camps were a scandal and a joke to other nations, and they were mostly rude and boorish, while the burghers and merchants whom they despised were well-read, thoughtful, cultivated people. Each prince and each city had fixed which form of doctrine should prevail. In the Lutheran ones the lands of the bishoprics and abbeys had been seized but in some of these the nunneries were kept up and called Chapters, as a home for ladies of noble birth, who took no vows, but enjoyed the estates.

Ferdinand would gladly have improved matters, but he was already an old man when he became Emperor, and he died in the year of 1564.

CHAPTER XXXI.

MAXIMILIAN II., ... 1564.

MAXIMILIAN II. was thirty-seven years of age when he succeeded his father. He was a kindly, warm-hearted man, beloved by all, and he allowed so much freedom to the Lutherans that he was sometimes accused of being one himself. He could speak six languages with ease, and King Henry III. of France declared that he was the most accomplished gentleman he ever met. He was so industrious that his chancellor said that if he had not been Emperor he would have been the best of chancellors, and he was always ready to hear the petitions of the meanest of his subjects. His Bohemian subjects said of him that they were as happy under him as if he had been their father, and all his people would have given the same character of him.

Unfortunately, whatever he did in his own dominions of Austria, Hungary, and Bohemia, he held little power over the princes of the Empire,

MAXIMILIAN II.

and they would not listen to his counsel. It had become the custom of the Germans to go forth as soldiers, calling themselves Landsknechts, and hiring themselves out to fight, no matter in what cause, provided they were well paid, and got plenty of plunder. This took them away from their proper work; there were not men enough left to till the ground, and such as came back were horribly idle, lawless, and wicked, unfit for a peaceful life. Maximilian tried to get the Diet to forbid the men of Germany from taking service with other princes, but he could not succeed, and Germans fought all through the wars in France and the Netherlands. However, the Diet agreed with the Kaisar in trying to put down the horrible lawlessness of some of the barons. There was a knight called Wilhelm of Grumbach who had ravaged Franconia with fire and sword, and had ended by murdering the Bishop of Wurtzburg. He had been put under the ban of the Empire, but Friedrich of Saxony, son of the deprived Elector, Johann Friedrich, thought proper to give him shelter at Gotha, and for seven years the edict could not be performed, but at last the Elector August came before Gotha with an army, and forced it to surrender, when Grumbach, after being barbarously tortured, was torn to pieces by wild horses, and Friedrich was imprisoned, and deprived of his lands, which were divided between his two sons.

Maximilian was a firm ally of Queen Elizabeth, and there was a plan at one time of one of his many sons marrying her, but this came to nothing. His daughter Elizabeth married Charles IX. of France, and was quite broken-hearted by the cruelties she saw at his court. Maximilian himself showed the greatest grief and indignation at the Massacre of St. Bartholomew, and always stood up for what was just and merciful.

His wife was Maria, daughter to Charles V., for the Austrian princes were far too apt to marry their cousins, and having no infusion of fresh spirit, the family became duller and duller, and none of the five sons of Maximilian were equal to himself. The third of them, who bore the same name as his father, was elected King of Poland by one party, but another party chose Siegmund of Sweden, and defeated him. Afterwards he was made Grand Master of the remains of the Teutonic Order. The estates of that Order in Eastern Prussia could not be recovered from the Elector of Brandenburg, to whom the Grand Master Albrecht had left them, for the Protestant princes mustered very strongly in the Diet, and would not give up a fragment of the Church lands which they had seized, and the

Emperor was determined not to go to war with them.

He was able to avoid war everywhere but in Hungary, where Johann Siegmund, Prince of Transylvania, attacked him, and was not ashamed to ask the aid of the terrible Sultan, Solyman the Magnificent. The enormous army of Turks advanced up the Danube, meaning to take Vienna itself, but they stopped to take the little town of Zagreth. Here the brave Count Zrini with 1500 men held out bravely. The place was in the middle of a bend of the river, and had strong walls, so that the Turks had to throw in earth to make roads, and raise mounds on which to plant their cannon. Even when they had battered down part of the walls, they were beaten back in nineteen assaults before at last they gained a footing in the outer part of the fortress. Only six hundred men were left within, and Count Zrini, seeing all hope gone, took the keys of the place, and with his father's sword in his hand sallied out at the head of his men, hoping to cut their way through the enemy. He was slain bravely fighting, and his men were driven back into the castle, and were there killed, all but a very few, whose wonderful bravery struck even the Turkish soldiers. They had stopped the Turks for a whole month, and their constancy was the saving of their country, for the long delay in the unwholesome marshes caused an illness, of which the Sultan, Solyman died, and thus the invasion was prevented. Peace was made with the new Sultan, Selim, and so honorable was the Emperor, that when a great league was made against the Turks by Spain, Venice, and the Pope, he would not join it, saying that a Christian could never be justified in breaking an oath. The allies defeated the Turkish fleet in the glorious sea-fight of Lepanto, and crushed their strength, but Maximilian forbade the Hungarians to make any great show of rejoicing, as he said it would be ungenerous to insult the Turks in their distress.

The crown of Poland was vacant again, and Maximilian proposed to the Poles to choose his third son, Ernst, a good, upright man, but with such low spirits that he was hardly ever seen to smile. The Poles would not have him, and chose instead the Emperor himself, a wise choice, for he was so much beloved that he was called by the Germans after the Emperor Titus, "the delight of the world."

Ernst's melancholy seems to have been inherited from the poor crazed Juana of Spain, grandmother to both Maximilian and his wife, and it often showed itself in both the Austrian and Spanish lines. Maximilian himself, though bright and cheerful, had never been strong, and he died suddenly while holding a diet at Regensburg, in his fiftieth year, on the 12th of October, 1576. His wife, with one of his daughters, then went into a convent in Spain. He had had sixteen children, of whom nine lived to grow up.

CHAPTER XXXII.

RUDOLF II., ... 1576–1612.

THE weakest and least sane of all the sons of Maximilian was the eldest, Rudolf, who had already been chosen King of the Romans, and succeeded his father in 1576. He was, however, in his early youth full of liveliness and cheerfulness, living, as his brothers said, too familiarly with people of all ranks; and he was a man of much reading, knowing many languages, and having a great turn for natural science, so that he formed botanical gardens, and collected a menagerie of foreign animals. He began the great museum of gems, statues, and pictures at Vienna, and encouraged learning, especially in Bohemia, where there were such good schools that most of the burghers were familiar with the old Greek and Latin poets. He also was very fond of chemistry and astronomy, and brought to his court the two men who had gone the farthest in the study of the stars, Tycho Brahe, a Swede, and Kepler, a Wurtemburgher.

In those days, however, chemistry and astronomy had two false sisters — alchemy, an endeavor to find the philosopher's stone, and therewith make gold; and astrology, which was supposed to foretell a man's fate by calculating the influences of the planets which stood foremost in the sky at his birth. These two vain studies seem to have turned Rudolf's head. An astrologer told him that he would die by the hand of one of the next generation of his own kindred; and to prevent this murderer from being born he would neither marry himself nor let any of his five brothers marry, except Albrecht, who would have seemed the most unlikely of all, since he was a Cardinal. As he had never really taken Holy Orders, he was chosen as the husband of Isabel Clara Eugenia, the daughter of Philip II. of Spain, and sent with her to govern Flanders, and what remained of the Netherlands after Holland and the other six provinces had broken loose from Philip II. Fear of the possible murder, however, grew on Rudolf, and he ceased to go out or hold audiences with his people, attend-

Rudolf and Tycho Brahe.

ing to nothing but his alchemy and his horses, of which he had a magnificent collection.

In the meantime things fell into disorder, and began to work towards a civil war. Germany was divided into three great parties — the Roman Catholics, of whom the chief was Maximilian, Duke of Bavaria; the Lutherans, whose principal leaders were the Electors, Johann Siegmund of Brandenburg and Johann George of Saxony; and the Calvinists, under Prince Christian of Anhalt and the Pfalzgraf or Elector Palatine of the Rhine.

The free city of Donauwerth was chiefly Protestant, but there was a Benedictine abbey within it, where the monks were undisturbed, on condition that they should make no processions. For many years they had refrained, but when the Rogation tide of 1605 came round, they went forth, as of old, to sing litanies and bless the crops. The magistrates stopped them, sent back the banners to the abbey, but let the procession go on. The Bishop of Wurtzburg complained to the Aulic Council, and a citation was sent to the magistrates, which, however, was placed in the Abbot's hands, and he did not show it till he found he was not to be allowed another procession. The magistrates tried to keep the peace, but the people had been worked up into a fury, and assaulted a funeral procession, destroying the banners and driving back the monks. On this Donauwerth was laid under the ban of the Empire, and the Duke of Bavaria was sent to carry it out. He did not act with violence, but marched into the city, which was able to make no resistance, restored the chief church to the Catholics, and united the city to his own duchy, to which it had formerly belonged.

The whole reformed party was offended, and formed into a great league. The Lutherans seem chiefly to have meant to keep all they had taken from the Church, but the Calvinists had hopes of depriving the House of Austria of the Empire. Maximilian of Bavaria formed a Catholic League in self-defence.

In the midst of these disturbances the Duke of Cleves died, and his duchy was disputed between the sons of his two sisters — the Elector of Brandenburg and young Duke Wolfgang of Neuburg. They were both Lutherans, and Wolfgang, at a conference between them, said the best way of settling the matter would be for him to marry his rival's daughter. The Elector was so angry at this proposal that he boxed the young man's ears, whereupon Wolfgang, in his anger, became a Roman

Catholic, and asked for help from Spain and Bavaria. On the other hand the Elector became a Calvinist, and was more active in the affairs of the union. The Emperor tried to interfere, but in vain, and the country of Julich and Cleves was divided between the two for a time.

In the meantime Rodolf's neglect of business had led to such confusion in both Austria and Hungary that they revolted against him, and forced him to give them up to his brother Matthias in 1606. Only Bohemia was left to him, and he hoped to keep that by putting forth a Letter of Majesty granting freedom of worship and equal rights to the Hussites and Protestants, but he allowed his cousin Leopold, Bishop of Passau, to raise an army in the Catholic interest. The Bohemians, seeing that he could not be trusted, called in Matthias, and deposed Rudolf, though they still allowed him his palace at Prague, where he could go on with his experiments with Tycho Brahe, who though a great astronomer, was as superstitious as himself. There was a comet in 1607, which the Emperor thought had come on his account. His fears of assassination increased. He would never go to church, or anywhere else except to his stables, and thither he had a passage made with oblique windows in the thickness of the wall to prevent being shot, and the whole lined with black marble, to show the reflection of any one who came near him. His own counsellors and foreign envoys had to disguise themselves as grooms to obtain a hearing, and he sometimes flew into violent rages on finding them out, while his fits of melancholy were worse than ever.

However, he roused himself to hold a meeting of the Electors at Nuremburg, told them how he was stripped and impoverished, and begged for a grant of revenues from the Empire. They showed him little pity, saying it was his own fault, and desiring to have a diet summoned for Electing any one of his brothers King of the Romans. This he felt to be a step towards taking away his last crown, and he kept on putting off and off the calling of the diet till the Electors lost patience, and summoned it for themselves.

This was the last blow. His depression increased, and he pined away till he found himself dying; then he brightened up, declaring that he felt as happy as when in his youth he had come home to Germany after a visit to Spain, for now he was going beyond the reach of change and sorrow. He died in the sixtieth year of his age, and the thirty-seventh of his reign, in the year 1612.

CHAPTER XXXIII.

MATTHIAS, ... 1612–1619.

THE new Emperor, Matthias, was a good and upright man, who had only taken part against his elder brother because he saw that otherwise the three hereditary states would be lost to the House of Hapsburg. So soon as he had freed himself from Rudolf's fancies, he had married his cousin, Anne of the Tyrol, whom he loved most tenderly, but he had no children — indeed the only one of all Maximilian's sixteen children who ever had a child was Anne, whose only child was Philip III. of Spain, and the Germans and Austrians alike would never have borne to pass under another Spanish King.

The fittest heir would thus be Ferdinand, Duke of Styria, who was son to Charles, a younger son of the Emperor, Ferdinand II. He had lost his father very early, and had been bred up by his Bavarian uncle and Jesuit teachers, so that he was a very devout and conscientious man, but not clever —and

MATTHIAS.

cold, shy, and grave. When, in 1596, he first came to take possession of his duchy, he found all the Styrians Protestants, and not one person in Grätz would receive the Holy Communion with him on Easter-day. He was so much shocked that he made a pilgrimage to Rome, and vowed to restore his duchy to the Church. He brought back a band of Capuchin Friars, and between their teaching and his own management he so entirely changed the profession of the Styrians that, in 1603, there were 40,000 at the Easter Mass.

This did not make the notion of him welcome to the Protestants. The Bohemians in especial had been meaning to keep quiet as long as Matthias lived, but on his death they meant to choose either the Elector of Saxony or the Elector Palatine. But in 1617 their diet was called together, and they were told that they had no right to choose any stranger, but must accept Ferdinand of Styria, to whom Matthias wished to resign the crown of Bohemia. They were taken by surprise, and did as they were bidden, though they believed their crown to be elective, and many of them were old Hussites.

Ferdinand doubted whether, as a good Catholic, he ought to swear to the Letter of Majesty granted by Rudolf, which made the Protestants equal with the Catholics, but the Jesuits told him that though it might have been wrong to grant it, it could not be wrong to accept it as part of the law of the land, and as he walked in state to his coronation, he said to one of his friends, "I am glad to have won this crown without any pangs of conscience."

However, he did not think himself bound to more than keeping the strictest letter of the law, while he believed it his duty to restore Bohemia to the Church. He banished all the Protestants and Hussite school-masters, founding two Convents of Capuchins and three Jesuit Colleges, and bringing in as many of his Catholics to settle in the country as possible. It was the plan that had succeeded in Styria, and there was very little resistance among the people in Bohemia. He was also elected King of Hungary, and there crowned, and a diet was soon to be assembled to appoint him King of the Romans.

His two chief Bohemian counsellors were Slavata and Martinitz, both zealous Catholics, whom he left as regents when he went to Germany; and on the opposite side was Count Thurm, a strong Lutheran, who hated the House of Hapsburg. A Lutheran church was pulled down, and the congregation was shut out of another because they did not come under the head of the Letter of Majesty. On this, Thurm and his friends sent a remonstrance to the Emperor, but Matthias justified all that his cousin had done, and they became afraid of absolute persecution. Thurm resolved to destroy the rule of the House of Hapsburg in Bohemia, and to begin by the death of the regents.

On the 23rd of May, 1618, a whole troop of Hussite and Lutheran armed nobles tramped up into the Council Chamber where Martinitz and Slavata were sitting, and reproached them with having been the authors of the Emperor's letter. A few hot words passed. "Let us follow the old custom, and hurl them from the window," some one cried; and they were dragged to a window seventy feet above the ditch of the Castle of Prague. Martinitz begged for a priest. "Commend thy soul to God," was the answer; "we will have no Jesuit scoundrels here;" and he was hurled out, uttering a prayer of which the murderers caught a few words, and one cried, "Let us see whether his Mary will help him." Slavata and the secretary were also hurled out, but, looking from the window, the man's next cry was, "His Mary has helped him." For there was a pile of waste paper just below, which had broken the fall, and all three crawled away unhurt.

This Defenestration, as the Bohemians called it,

was in truth the beginning of the Thirty Years' War which ravaged Germany, and threw back all progress and improvement all the time it lasted, and bred some of the most savage and lawless soldiers who ever drew sword. The Hussites began it in real fear for their religion, and also feeling that the nation had been cheated by the House of Austria of the power of electing their king, and they hoped for help from the Lutheran and Calvinist princes who had any quarrel with that family. They wrote a letter justifying their treatment of the two regents by the fate of Jezebel, and raised almost all Bohemia against Ferdinand.

The Emperor Matthias had enough of the spirit of his father to wish to win them back by gentle means, and his chief adviser, Cardinal Klesel, was fully of the same mind. They tried to hold back Ferdinand, who wanted to take speedy vengeance, and was supported by his former guardian, the Archduke Maximilian, and the Jesuits. When they found that the Emperor would not send troops from the Spanish Netherlands to reduce Bohemia, these two princes caused Klesel to be seized, stripped of his robes, and sent off a prisoner to a castle in the Tyrol. Matthias was ill in bed with gout, and when his brother went and told him what had been done, his wrath and grief were so great that he could not trust himself to speak, but thrust the bed-clothes into his mouth till he was almost choked. He was too feeble and old to hinder Ferdinand from sending Spanish and Flemish troops into Bohemia, but Count Thurn was at

FRIEDRICH V

the head of ten thousand insurgents, and had allied himself with Bethlem Gabor, Waiwode of Transylvania, and with the Protestant Union, at the head of which was the Elector Palatine, Friedrich, the husband of Elizabeth, daughter of James I. of England.

The Catholic Germans were for the most part of the same mind as the Emperor, ready to do anything to prevent war, and Matthias getting better, fixed a meeting at Egra to try to come to some agreement, but his wife died just then, and he sank into a state of depression, comparing his cousin's usage of him to his own treatment of his brother Rudolf, and grieving over the miseries he saw coming on the Empire. He died before the conference could take place, on the 20th of March, 1619.

CHAPTER XXXIV.

THE REVOLT OF BOHEMIA.

FERDINAND II., ... 1619-1621.

AFFAIRS were in a very unpromising state for Ferdinand when Matthias died. The Protestant princes of the Union were unwilling to make him Emperor, nor would the Bohemians accept his promise to renew the Letter of Majesty, but Count Thurm, by favor of the numerous Austrian Protestants, marched up to the very walls of Vienna.

Ferdinand sent his wife and children away to the Tyrol, and waited at Vienna himself with only three hundred men whom he could depend upon. The Austrians meant to profit by his distress, and insisted that he should accept a charter which united them with the Bohemians, and made them far too strong for his reforms. He threw himself on his knees, and prayed for aid to stand firm against what his conscience forbade, and he thought he heard a voice in answer, "Fear not, I will not forsake thee."

The Bohemian cannon were firing on his palace, and sixteen Austrian nobles rushed in on him, calling on him to sign the charter, telling him that the city had revolted, and that if he did not sign he should be shut up in a convent, and his children should be bred up Protestants. One noble even took him roughly by the button of his coat, saying, "Sign it, Nandel!" but he never lost his firmness, and at that moment a trumpet was heard outside. A troop of Flemish horse, sent to Ferdinand's aid by the Archduke Albert, had entered by a gate not guarded by Thurm, and he was rescued.

The Bohemians retreated, and proceeded to hold a diet at Prague, where they elected the Elector Palatine, Friedrich, as their king. He was at that time at the Diet of the Empire. The three Protestant Electors had much rather not have chosen Ferdinand, but as they could agree on no one else, the three Archbishops led them, and there was no vote against him.

The Elector Palatine was advised against accept-

Ferdinand II.

ing the Bohemian crown by his father-in-law, James
I., who said he must not reckon on English aid in
meddling with other people's rights, and his own
mother was of the same mind. He himself was
weak and perplexed. "If I refuse," he said, "I
shall be accused of cowardice; if I accept, of ambi-
tion. Decide as I may, all is over for me and my
country." But his wife, Elizabeth Stewart, thought
acceptance a duty, and taunted him with having
married a king's daughter without spirit to act as
a king, and, half distracted, he yielded, and set off
from his beautiful home in Heidelberg amid the
tears of all his people. On the 4th of November,
1619, he was crowned at Prague, where he was
received with great joy. The ladies sent Elizabeth
sacks of all sorts of cakes, and an ebony cradle
inlaid with silver for her son Rupert, her third
child, who was born the next month. But Friedrich was such a Calvinist as soon to offend the
Hussites, who had kept all the old ornaments on
their churches, and had the Catholic service in
their own tongue. He also quarreled with Count
Thurm, and gave command of the army to Prince
Christian of Anhalt.

"Here is a prince in a fine labyrinth," said the
Pope, and "He will be only a winter king," said

the Jesuits. And in the spring the Flemish army entered the Palatinate, and horribly ravaged the beautiful Rhineland, so that the Electress dowager and her grandchildren could hardly escape. Maximilian of Bavaria, at the head of an army of his own people and of Austrians, entered Bohemia, and Count Tilly, the chief Austrian general, encamped on the White Hill above Prague. It was a Sunday morning, and the Gospel read for the day was — "Render unto Cæsar the things that are Cæsar's." The soldiers took it as a good omen, and Tilly gave battle as soon as mass was over.

Friedrich was at dinner with the English envoys when he heard that his men were flying, and Anhalt fled into the town bare-headed to say that all was lost. The gates were opened, a carriage brought to the door, Friedrich and Elizabeth hurried into it, little Rupert was thrown into the bottom of it, and they drove away, to find a refuge at last at the Hague, among the Dutch. The Bohemians were at the mercy of the Catholic League under Maximilian and Tilly. The whole country was ravaged, multitudes of peasants were slain, the nobles were beheaded, and all the old Hussite churches given to the Catholics, while the ministers were banished. Priests, friars, and Jesuits were sent to instruct the people, and before the end of the reign the Hussite and Lutheran doctrine had been trampled out in Bohemia.

Friedrich of the Rhine was put to the ban of the Empire, and Maximilian of Bavaria was made Elector in his stead. He might have saved the remains of his County Palatine if he would have taken the advice of King James, who tried to mediate for him, and have ceased to call himself King of Bohemia; but he would not do this, and Count Peter Mansfeld still held two Bohemian towns for him, and having no money, his soldiers lived by horrible pillage and rapine. The Protestant Union, though they had disapproved of the attack on Bohemia, did not choose to lose an Elector from their number, and undertook the defence of Friedrich. Moreover, Elizabeth was so beautiful and spirited, that the young princes who saw her grew ardent in her cause, and the young Christian of Brunswick called himself her knight, and wore her glove in his helmet, with the inscription. "For God and for her." He was a younger son of the Duke of Brunswick, but a Lutheran, and had been provided for with a bishopric for the sake of the estates, though he was nothing but a soldier. But this was the way the Lutheran princes dealt with the old Bishoprics.

With Tilly commanding the Catholic Germans and Spinola the Flemings on the Emperor's side, and Anhalt, Mansfeld, and Brunswick the Protestants, the war began to rage on the Palatinate on the banks of the Rhine. Tilly was a Hungarian of peasant birth, brave and honest, but very fierce and rude. He went to battle in a green slashed coat, and slouched hat with a red feather, and was brutal with his soldiers, and unmerciful to the enemy. This thirty years' war was one of the most horrible ever known. The soldiers were chiefly men trained to fight as a trade from their youth up, coming from every nation, hiring themselves out for a certain time, and serving only for pay and plunder, with no real feeling for their cause, and no pity for man, woman, or child. Their generals looked to maintain them by pillage, and to wear out the enemy by ruining his country. "Burning-masters" were officers in their armies, and horror and misery came wherever they went.

CHAPTER XXXV.

GUSTAF ADOLF AND WALLENSTEIN.

FERDINAND II., ... 1621–1634.

AFTER Tilly had defeated Mansfeld and Christian of Brunswick, the war seemed dying away, but Christian II., King of Denmark, took up the cause of the German Protestants, and entered Saxony, joined Mansfeld, who had raised another army. The Elector Johann George would not join them, but he would not help the Emperor, because Ferdinand resisted the giving away of Bishoprics to young Lutheran princes.

Maximilian of Bavaria and Count Tilly were ready to fight for the Empire and the Church, but Ferdinand wanted a general and an army more entirely his own, and yet he had no money to raise troops. Just then there came forward Count

Albrecht von Waldstein, or Wallenstein, as he came to be called, a Bohemian noble, who as a lad had become a Roman Catholic, but had more faith in astrology than in any religion, and could be led to anything that he thought his star directed. He had become very rich by buying up the estates forfeited by the Bohemian nobles, and he came to the Emperor and offered to raise an army of 50,000 men, and make it support itself, not by plunder, but by forcing contributions from the states it occupied.

Ferdinand thought this not so bad as plunder, and consented, creating Wallenstein Duke of Friedland. He soon raised his army, chiefly from disbanded men of the Protestant army. He beat Mansfeld first on the Elbe, and the King of Denmark on the Lutter. Then the duchy of Holstein, which belonged to Denmark, but was part of the German Empire, was taken from the King, and Wallenstein was rewarded by being made Duke of Mecklenburg and Generalissimo of the Empire by sea and land. Afterwards, he tried to enter Stralsund on the Baltic, a free city, and one of the Hanse towns, and when he found the gates closed, he besieged it, declaring, "I will have the city, though it were bound with chains of adamant to heaven." The magis-

Wildenstein Castle

trates appealed to the Emperor, who commanded him to give up the siege, but he paid no attention, and went on with the attack. However, the Kings of Sweden and Denmark sent aid to the Stralsunders, and he had to retire, after having lost many men.

He had grown so proud and powerful that his state and splendor surpassed those of the princes, and the Catholic League, with the Elector of Bavaria at its head, pressed Ferdinand to dismiss him for his disobedience and presumption in attacking a free city, declaring that unless this was done, they would not choose the Emperor's son King of the Romans.

The French minister Richelieu, who wanted to ruin Ferdinand, was playing a double game, persuading the Emperor to give up his general, and at the same time advising the princes against electing young Ferdinand, while he tried to stir up fresh enemies for the House of Austria. The Duke of Friedland then retired to his estates, where he lived more splendidly than most kings of his time. He was waited on by nobles, and had sixty highborn pages and fifty life-guards waiting in his own chamber; his table was never laid for less than a hundred; and when he traveled it was with sixty carriages and one hundred wagons. He hated noise so much, that when he was at Prague he had chains put across the streets near his palace that

GUSTAF ADOLF.

nothing might disturb him, and his study, where he spent much time in observing the stars, and drawing omens from them, was a wonderful place. His manner was blunt, short, and proud, but there was something about him that, together with his magnificent gifts, bound men's hearts to him.

Ferdinand, having thus gained the victory, insisted that the Church property belonging to bishoprics and abbeys should be given up. Again the Protestants felt themselves aggrieved, and their defence was taken up by Gustaf Adolf, King of Sweden, the noblest man and best soldier of the age, and one of its truest Christians.

He kept his army in perfect order, and would allow no plunder or violence, taking care that his men should be well fed, clothed, and lodged, and giving them chaplains, who read prayers and taught them. He came in the spirit of one who hoped to work a deliverance for his religion, and as he entered Pomerania in 1630, all were amazed at his orderly army, paying its way and doing no harm. The Catholics called him the Snow-king, who would melt as he came southwards, and Tilly marched to oppose him.

The free town of Magdeburg was Protestant. Tilly besieged it, and took it by assault before Gustaf could come to save it. Then there was the most horrible sack ever known, while the savage soldiers murdered, robbed, drank, rioted, and burnt, more like fiends than human beings, and Tilly called this their reward. The fire drove them out at last, when out of 40,000 inhabitants only 800 were left.

These atrocities horrified all Germany. Many princes who had doubted before now joined Gustaf, and he fought a great battle at Leipsic with Tilly, and routed him completely. It was the old general's first defeat out of thirty battles, and it opened Gustaf's way into south Germany. Marching towards Bavaria, he met Tilly again, on the banks of the Lech, and was again victorious, Tilly being killed by a shot in the leg. Gustaf would have restored Friedrich to Heidelberg on condition that he would give Lutherans equal rights with Calvinists, but this he would not do, and three months later he died of a fever.

All the free towns received Gustaf joyfully, and he marched into Bavaria, while Maximilian fled to Regensburg. At Munich, the burghers received the conqueror on their knees, but he bade them rise, saying, "Kneel to God, not man." He allowed no plunder, and left the Elector's palace and stores of pictures untouched. All he wanted was the cannon, and these were found buried under-

Death of Wallenstein.

ground, and the largest of all stuffed to the muzzle with gold pieces.

Meantime the Elector of Saxony was overrunning Bohemia, but Wallenstein had been roused to take the command again, and he hunted the Elector back to Saxony. There Gustaf came to his help, and at Lutzen, in November, 1632, these two great generals fought a great battle. The Swede was the victor, but was killed in the midst of the fight, it is much feared by the treachery of a German Duke. A monument, called the Stone of the Swede, marks where he fell — the best and greatest man of his time. Young Duke Bernard of Saxe Weimar, a brave and good young man, took the command, but he could not keep Gustaf's discipline, and his army was soon as great a scourge as Mansfeld's had been.

Wallenstein had gone into Bohemia, and there would obey no orders either from the Emperor or the Elector of Bavaria. When he was reproved, he made all his chief officers sign a bond to hold fast by him whatever happened. This was flat treason, and some, though signing it, sent information to the Emperor, and then left him. He now began to deal with the other side, and offered to give the city of Egra up to the Protestants. Bernhard would have nothing to do with such a traitor, but the other allies listened, and Egra was just about to be delivered up by Wallenstien, when six Scottish and Irish officers of his guards resolved to hinder the deed by his death. Just as he had gone to bed, they broke into his rooms, as he met them at the door he was slain at once by six halberts in his breast, on the 25th of February, 1634.

CHAPTER XXXVI.

FERDINAND II., ... 1634–1637.
FERDINAND III................ 1637.

ON the death of Wallenstein, the command of the Catholic army was given to the Emperor's son Ferdinand, who had been chosen King of Hungary and Bohemia, and to his aid came the Governor of the Low Countries, a son of the King of Spain, commonly called the Cardinal Infant, who, church dignitary though he was, was a brave captain. Together, they gave the Protestants a terrible defeat at Nordlingen, and the party was beginning to fall to pieces. The Germans hated the Swedes, the Swedes were jealous of Bernhard of Saxe Weimar, and all began to consider of peace, for the war was growing more dreadful than ever. The soldiers on both sides were worse than savages, and found their pleasure in torture for its own sake, sticking needles into the miserable people who fell into their hands, sawing their flesh to the bone, scalding them with hot water, or hunting them with dogs. Whole villages in Brandenburg and Saxony lay utterly waste, with no living creature in them but the famished dogs that prowled

BERNHARD OF SAXE WEIMAR

round the desolate hearths, and along the road lay dead bodies with a little grass in their mouths.

The English Ambassador on his way to Prague saw many such sights, and fed many starving wretches on his way. One poor little village which he passed through had been pillaged twenty-eight times in two years!

He was going to a conference at Prague, where there was an attempt to make peace, but every one was displeased with the terms, and the French, who had been hoping all along to get something for themselves out of the misfortunes of Germany, and had set their hearts on the province of Elsass, declared war against the Empire just before the peace was signed between Ferdinand and the princes of the Empire. Bernhard of Saxe Weimar was invited to Paris, and much admired and caressed. He was made a general both in the French and in the Swedish armies, and now the war was not between Catholic and Protestant Germans, but between Germans on the one hand, and Swedes and French on the other; for the Swedes were fighting for the duchy of Pomerania, which had been promised to the Elector of Brandenburg.

In the midst died Ferdinand II., on the 15th of February, 1637. He was a good and devout man, but narrow-minded, and so much devoted to the Jesuits and Capuchins that his confessor said of him, that if an angel and a monk gave him contrary advice, he believed he would take the monk's. He was most kind and charitable, and would wait on beggars and lepers with his own hands, and he was much beloved by his Catholic subjects.

His son, Ferdinand III., was very like him. His great love was for keeping accounts, and he did save a great deal of money, but he wrote such a bad hand that when he sent orders to his generals they could always avoid obeying them, by declaring they could not read them. His reign began in the midst of the weary old war, the Swedes fighting for Pomerania, and the French for Elsass. Bernhard of Saxe Weimer took Brisach, fancying Elsass would be given to him, and he was angered and disappointed when he found this was the last thing the French thought of. He set off to make his way to the Swedes, who were overrunning Brandenburg, but on the way he caught a fever, and died in 1639, when only thirty-six years old, worn out by the miserable war, and grief at the atrocities he could not prevent. In the midst of his illness he heard that the enemy were attacking the camp, and rising from his sick-bed, he mounted his horse and drove them back.

All the Germans, Catholic and Protestant, were united now, and they had the Spaniards to help them, but the French and Swedes were both under able generals. The Swedish Count Banier won so many victories that six hundred standards of his taking are still in the Cathedral at Stockholm. Hungary was attacked by George Bagotsky of Transylvania, and Germany by the French, who won two terrible battles at Friburg and Nordlingen, and had orders to march into Bavaria and lay the country waste.

This threat was to force the Elector Maximilian to make a separate peace with France. He was the only one left of all the princes who had been living at the beginning of the war, and had upheld the cause of the Emperor all through, but he could not give up his country to the savage soldiers, and he signed a truce. The Emperor, losing his help, was in greater straits than ever, the Swedes overran Bohemia, and one night broke into the Emperor's camp, and killed the sentries before his tent. When the truce was over, Maximilian joined Ferdinand again. The last great battle of the war was fought at Zusmarschenen, in 1648, with the Swedes, who again gained a great victory. Bavaria was overrun and laid waste, and in Bohemia, half Prague was taken by them.

At Prague the war had begun in 1618, at Prague it ended in 1648. Germany was worn out; it had only half the inhabitants it had at the beginning of the war. Many towns were in ruins, many villages deserts, trade was destroyed, misery everywhere. The old Hanse League had fallen to pieces because the once wealthy cities could not pay their expenses. Peace must be made; so a congress was held at Münster in Westphalia, and attended by deputies from all parts of Europe. The two foreign enemies were bought off—France with Elsass, and Sweden with half Pomerania. The other half went to the Elector of Brandenburg, also the bishopric of Magdeburg; Bavaria had the lower Palatinate, but the upper Palatinate was restored to Karl Ludwig, the son of the Winter King, and brother of Rupert, who had been fighting for his uncle, Charles I., in England. At the same time Holland, the Netherlands, and Switzerland were declared free, and independent of the Empire.

As to religious matters, all benefices that had been in Catholic or Protestant hands in 1624 were so to remain, the Imperial Council was to be of equal numbers of Catholics and Protestants, each prince might enforce what religion he pleased on his subjects, and Calvinism was as much recognized as Lutheranism. Nobody liked the terms of this peace, but everybody was so worn out that it was agreed to. Thenceforth, then, the great outlines were

Peace of Westphalia.

settled. Austria, Hungary, Tyrol, and Bohemia, being the hereditary lands of the Emperor, were Catholic, also Bavaria; while Brandenburg, Saxony, Brunswick, and most of the northern states and free cities were Protestant, and though the Empire still existed, all the princes were much more independent of it. Maximilian of Bavaria died in 1651, three years after the peace was signed, much respected for the faithful, honest part he had acted. The Emperor lived till 1657. He was not an able man, but he had never throughout his reign done a single act that he knew to be unjust. When he was sitting in his room, weak and ill, the nurses rushed in with his youngest child's cradle, because the nursery was on fire, and in their fright knocked the cradle against the wall, so that it was broken, and the child fell out. The shock so startled the father that he only lived an hour after, and the baby died of the fall a few months later.

CHAPTER XXXVII.

THE SIEGE OF VIENNA.

LEOPOLD I., ... 1657-1687.

THE eldest son of Ferdinand III. died before his father, and the second, Leopold, was not eighteen, and had not yet been chosen King of the Romans. This gave Louis XIV. of France an opportunity of trying to get himself elected to the Empire, and he gained over the three Electoral Archbishops and the Elector Palatine, who had become a Roman Catholic, but Friedrich Wilhelm of Brandenburg, who is called the Great Elector, kept the others firm against France, and Leopold was chosen. He had been educated for the priesthood, and was a very devout and good man, most upright and careful, but he was far from clever or strong, and could not do great things, though he did little things, very well. He was so good a player on the violin that his music master exclaimed—" What a pity your majesty is not a fiddler!"

He was unfortunate, for Louis XIV. was on the

LEOPOLD I.

watch to gain all he could from Germany in its worn-out state, and was his enemy all his life, leaguing with the Rhineland princes against him, so that the war began again.

The Great Elector saw through Louis's plans, and did his best to keep the Germans together, but the Swedes invaded his part of Pomerania, and he had to fight with them, when he not only drove them back, but seized most of what they had been granted at the peace of Münster.

The Austrians were defeated on the Rhine and a peace was made at Nimeguen in 1678 for all Europe, when Brandenburg was forced to give up what he had gained in Pomerania.

In spite of the peace, Louis declared that the great free city of Strasburg belonged to Elsass, and in 1681, while most of the burghers were away at the great fair of Frankfort, he seized the place, and kept it, bribing the chief inhabitants to submit, and changing it as much as possible to be a French Roman Catholic instead of a German Protestant city.

The Germans were furious, and would have made a league to recover it, but that the Elector of Brandenburg was so angry at having been deprived of his conquest in Pomerania that he would not join the Emperor in anything. Moreover, Louis stirred up the Hungarians against him, and indeed

Leopold had been very harsh to the Protestants there, and had sent two hundred and fifty of their pastors to row as galley slaves at Naples, where the great Dutch Admiral Denyter obtained their freedom. The Hungarians revolted, and after a few years called in to their aid Mahommed IV., the Sultan who sent his Grand Vizier, Kara Mustafa, at the head of 200,000 men, to invade Austria itself. Leopold and his family were obliged to take flight, and left Vienna to be defended by the governor, Count Starenburg, and its bishop, Kolonitsch, who had been a Knight of St. John, with a small, brave garrison. Outside was the Austrian army, under the Duke of Lorraine, with such an army as he could collect, and in it the young Prince Eugene, a cousin of the Duke of Savoy. He had been bred up at the French Court, but he had grown weary of its stiffness, and ran away with some other young men to fight against the Turks. Their letters were captured and opened, and were found to make game of the King. He never forgave what was said of him, and Eugene continued to serve the Emperor. But the Duke of Lorraine was not strong enough to fight the Turks, and Vienna was almost starved, so that the people had to eat dogs, rats, and cats (which they call d roofpares). The only hope was in Poland, which for once had a really great man for its King, named John Sobieski. He was collecting his troops to come to the aid of the Austrians, and much were they longed for. The Turks outside had grown so weary of the siege that they were heard crying, "O ye infidels, if ye will not come yourselves, let us at least see your crests over the hills, for then the siege will be over, and we shall be free."

To lessen their discontent, Kara Mustafa ordered an assault to be made. It was beaten off, but such was the loss of men, and such damage was done to the walls, that the Viennese thought their doom was come. On what they feared would be their last night, Starenburg sent up a volley of rockets from the tower of the Cathedral. Behold, it was answered by five more from Kohlenberg hill! Then he knew that help was at hand, and sent a messenger to swim across the Danube by night with a letter to the Duke of Lorraine with these few words — "No time to be lost. No time indeed to be lost."

Lorraine and Sobieski joined their forces, and burst down from the hills upon the enemy. When the Turks saw that all hope was vain, they murdered every captive in their hands and all their own women who could not be carried away, but they left the babies, and five hundred of these poor little things were brought to the good Bishop, who had them baptized and brought up at his own expense. An immense quantity of stores were taken, among them so much coffee that it then became a common drink, and the first coffee-house in Europe was opened by the same man who had swum the Danube.

Sobieski rode into Vienna with the people thronging round to kiss his horse and his sword, and calling him father and deliverer. Leopold was too proud to be grateful, and was half jealous, half afraid. He came into Vienna barefoot, with a taper in his hand, and went straight to the Cathedral, but he would not see Sobieski till he had made up his mind what ceremonies to observe. "How should an Emperor meet a King of Poland?" he asked. "With open arms," said the Duke of Lorraine.

They did meet on horseback outside the city, and Leopold said a few cold words in Latin, but was so uncivil that the Polish army was very angry, and the Duke of Lorraine and his Germans were shocked — nor would Leopold allow the Polish sick to be brought into the city, nor those who died to be buried in the churchyards. However, Sobieski still fought on, hunted the Turks back to the Danube, and together with the Duke of Lorraine gained a great victory at Gran, which delivered that city from the Turks after they had held it eighty years.

The Emperor began to punish the Hungarians, whose revolt had caused this invasion. He set up a tribunal at Eperies, where a fierce Italian named Caraffa acted as judge, and sent out parties of horse to bring in all who were supposed not to wish well to the House of Austria. They were accused of conspiracy, tortured, and put to death so ruthlessly that the court was known as the Shambles of Eperies. After this, he took away from the Hungarians the right of electing their king, declaring the crown to be hereditary in his own family, and sending his eldest son, Joseph, at ten years old, to be crowned at Presburg with the crown of St. Stephen. He promised the nobles all their former rights, and engaged to abolish the tribunal of Eperies if they would agree to own that their kingdom was hereditary both in the male and female line, but they held out for the right of choosing a new family if the male line of Hapsburgs should end, and Leopold gave way, not seeing much chance as yet of sons being wanting to his house. This was in 1687.

CHAPTER XXXVIII.

WAR OF THE SUCCESSION.

LEOPOLD I.,............... 1635–1705.

IN 1605 had died Karl, the Elector Palatine, grandson to the Winter King. He left no children, and his nearest male relations, the Duke of Neuburg, father to the Empress, inherited the county on the Rhine, but Elizabeth, the sister of the late Pfalzgraf, was married to the Duke of Orleans, brother to Louis XIV., and the French king hoped through her to gain more of the border of the river. So he claimed as her right various Rhineland fortresses, which would have let the French quite into the heart of the country. When the claim was refused, Marshal Duras was sent to invade the country, with orders to destroy what he could not keep. It was the depth of winter, and three days' notice was given to each unhappy village that the people might remove, and then every house was pillaged and burnt, every garden rooted up, and even the vineyards and corn-fields laid waste. Wurms and Mannheim were burnt, the tombs of the German emperors at Spiers were broken open, and the noble old castle of Heidelberg was blown up with gunpowder.

It was worse than even Louis XIV. had intended, and he stopped the ruin that was intended for Trier, but the Markgraf of Baden declared that he had come from Hungary only to see that Christians could be more savage than Turks.

In the midst of this horrible war died the Great Elector Friedrich Wilhelm of Brandenburg, after having ruled for forty-eight years, and having restored Brandenburg and Prussia to prosperity after the dreadful state in which the Thirty Years' War had left them.

The Elector of Saxony, August, had, on Sobieski's death, become a Roman Catholic, because he wanted to be King of Poland. He was a man of such wonderful strength that he could twist a horseshoe into any shape he pleased with his fingers, but he was a bad and dissipated man, whose profusion was quite a proverb, and whose vice was frightful. One gypsying party alone cost 3,000,000 dollars!

The Protestants complained so much that his defection upset the balance of the diet that they were allowed another Elector, Ernst August, Duke of Brunswick-Luneburg, who had become Elector of Hanover.

The war in the Palatinate was, however, not so much fought out in Germany as by the Emperor's allies, the other powers of Europe, with William III. of England as their leading spirit, and in 1697 peace was made at Ryswick, leaving Strasburg to France, but taking back to Germany Briesach, Friburg, and Philipsburg, which had been seized as belonging to Elsass.

But the peace of Ryswick was only a resting-time before another war which every one saw coming, since Carlos II., King of Spain, was a sickly man, without children, whose death was constantly expected — and what was to become of his kingdom? He had no brother, but he had two sisters: the eldest had married Louis XVI., who had left a son; the other, Margarita, had been the first wife of Leopold, and had left one daughter, Antonio, who had married the Elector of Bavaria, and had a son named Ferdinand.

Friedrich I, King of Prussia (Coronation).

The mothers of Leopold and Louis had also been Spanish princesses. France was so much too powerful already that the powers of Europe could not let the Dauphin inherit Spain — besides, his mother had renounced her rights to Spain on becoming Queen of France. So the right heir seemed to be young Ferdinand of Bavaria, and Carlos made his will in his favor, but this had scarcely been done before the boy died, and the French and Austrians accused one another of poisoning him. Leopold's second wife, Eleonore of Neuburg, one of the best and most devout women in Europe, had given him two sons, Joseph and Karl, and he declared that all rights of the French queen having been renounced, he was the next heir through his mother, and that he would make over his claim to his second son, Karl; and to make sure of the support of the German powers, he offered to make the Electors of Brandenburg and Saxony kings. Friedrich of Brandenburg, who was a weak man, fond of show and finery, was delighted. He chose to be called King of Prussia, and went to great expense for his coronation, but his wife was a very clever woman, who used to study with the philosopher Leibnitz, and was heartily weary of all his pomp and show. Louis XIV. promised to be contented with the duchy of Lorraine and kingdom of **Naples** and Sicily, and leave Karl Spain and the Netherlands, and the other nations swore to see this carried out. But poor Carlos II. thought it his duty to leave his kingdom to his nearest relation, and when he died, in 1700, he was found to have left all by will to Philip, Duke of Anjou, the second grandson of Louis XIV., and he was at once sent off to take possession, while the Elector of Bavaria and his brother, the Archbishop of Köln, sided with him. However, the Emperor began the war in Italy, whither he sent Prince Eugene, who was by far his best general. He was a little lean man — a strange figure in his blue coat, brass buttons, and enormous cocked hat, but he was greatly respected for his uprightness, bravery, and skill, and he brought over his cousin, the Duke of Savoy, to take the Austrian instead of the French side.

The Archduke Karl was sent to try his fortune in Spain, where he prospered as long as the English Lord Peterborough fought for him, but his German advisers were so dull and wrong-headed, and he himself so proud and stupid, that Peterborough threw up his command, and then the French gained ground, and Karl was forced to shut himself up in Barcelona.

Marlborough and Eugene.

In the meantime, the Elector Maximilian of Bavaria had brought a whole French army into his duchy to invade the Austrian Tyrol, which Bavaria always coveted. He gained some successes at first, but the Tyrolese, always the most true and loyal of peasants, drove him out with great loss. Eugene had been called back from Italy, and an English army, under the great Duke of Marlborough, marched up from Holland. These two great men then began a warm friendship, which never slackened, and together they met the huge French army which had come to aid Bavaria, and utterly routed it — first at Dónauwerth, and then at Hochstadt, or, as the English call it, Blenheim, making the French general, Tallard, a prisoner on the 13th of August, 1701.

It was the first victory gained over the French since the battle of St. Quentin, and it drove them quite out of Bavaria, which was held by the Austrian troops, while the Elector fled into the Netherlands.

Leopold had only just lived to see the tide turn, and his great enemy, Louis, begin to lose. He was already out of health, and died on the 5th of May, 1705. He was sometimes called the Thick-lipped, the large upper lip inherited with the Tyrol from

Margarethe Maultasch being specially visible in him. He was in some ways like the Emperor Rudolf, being very studious and learned, and also so shy that his nobles hardly knew him by sight. One of his chamberlains, who was seldom at the palace, met a little dark figure in a passage, and asked, "Where's the Kaisar?" "That am I," answered a hoarse voice. The Empress Eleonore survived him fifteen years, always busy in works of piety and charity, so that she was called "the mother of the poor." When she died, she bade these words alone to be inscribed on her coffin — "Eleonore, a poor sinner, died 19th January, 1720."

CHAPTER XXXIX.

JOSEPH I., ... 1705–1711.

JOSEPH, the eldest son of Leopold I., was twenty-six when he became Emperor. He was a very sensible and able man, superior to most of his family. He was fair and handsome, and was learned in many languages, with much knowledge of art and science; he was also much more free and ready of speech and manner than his father, though he hated fine speeches, and would not attend to birthday odes. "I come to hear music, not my own praise," he said, when these began in the theatre.

He took away some of the harsh decrees against the Protestants who remained in his hereditary dominions, and he forbade the Catholic priests to preach sermons abusing them, and in everything he gave his chief confidence to Prince Eugene, to whom he looked up like a father.

War was going on everywhere. The Bavarians had revolted against the Austrians, and called back their Elector with the help of the French and there was a sharp war before he was driven out again, and put to the ban of the Empire.

Then August of Saxony, as King of Poland, had, in alliance with Russia, made war on the young King Charles XII. of Sweden, and had thus brought down on himself a most terrible enemy, for Charles was one of the most fierce and stern of warriors, less like a man than a piece of iron wound up to do nothing but fight. He drove August out of Poland, hunted him up and down Saxony, beat him over and over again, and would not grant him any respite unless he would resign the crown of Poland, and give up other matters very dear to him. August begged to see Charles, in hopes of softening him, but the Swede, to show contempt for the shameful luxury he found in the palace at Dresden, would talk of nothing but his great jack-boots, telling the other king that he never took them off save when he went to bed. He stayed a year in Saxony, and settled the affairs of Poland by making king a young nobleman named Stanislas Lecksinsky, after which he marched off to Russia, where he found the Czar, Peter the Great, much too strong for him.

The war of the Spanish succession was going on

JOSEPH I.

all the time, though the Archduke Karl was unable to hold any ground in Spain; Marlborough was fighting the French in the Netherlands, and Eugene was sent by Joseph to help his cousin of Savoy, whose lands were being terribly ravaged by the French.

His capital, Turin, was being besieged, when Eugene brought up the Austrian army, and attacked the French in their camp, gaining such a victory, that out of 50,000 men only 20,000 were left by the time the broken army arrived at Pignerol, and the French were entirely driven out of Lombardy. Then Eugene marched even to the kingdom of Naples, where the people were quite willing to cast off the dominion of Philip of France; and after this, Eugene and Victor Amadeus advanced into the old Imperial fief of Provence, and laid seige to Toulon, but could not take it. The House of Austria had never so prospered since the days of Charles V., and Eugene, going to join Marlborough in the Netherlands, shared in another great victory at Oudenarde.

After all these losses Louis XIV. began to beg for peace, but Joseph and Queen Anne of England would only consent on condition that he should help to drive his own grandson out of Spain, and this was too much to ask, so the war raged on, and the allied armies in Flanders laid seige to Lille, which had excellent fortifications, and was defended by the brave Marshal Boufflers. Eugene managed the siege, while Marlborough protected him. Two assaults were beaten off, and Eugene was once struck on the head by a splinter, and was thought to be killed. At last Boufflers gave up the town, and retired into the citadel, hoping in vain to be relieved, but the French army would not venture on a battle, and a letter was sent to Boufflers allowing him to surrender. There was no way of sending it but through the Austrian army, and Eugene himself forwarded it with a note telling the brave Boufflers how much he admired his defence, and that he might choose his own terms. Boufflers offered what he thought fair, and this was accepted. He asked Eugene to dine with him, and the answer was — "I will come if you will give me one of your siege dinners;" and so the first course consisted entirely of horse-flesh, dressed in different ways.

The next year there was another terrible battle at Malplaquet, still in the Netherlands, and harder fought than any had been before, though the French were again beaten. In the course of the battle Eugene was wounded in the knee, but he would not leave the field, saying that if he lived till evening there would be time to dress wounds then.

But in this full tide of success a grievous blow fell upon Germany. Joseph caught the smallpox, and, according to the treatment of the time, was rolled up in twenty yards of scarlet cloth, with every breath of air shut out from his room, so that it was no wonder that he died in his thirty-third year, on the 17th of April, 1711. His only son had died when a few months old, and he had only two daughters; so he left his hereditary states to his brother, making him sign what was called the Family Compact, that if he too should have no male heir, Joseph's daughter should come before his in the succession.

The war was, under Marlborough and Eugene, carried on in a much less savage manner, but the little courts of Germany were mostly in a very bad state. August of Saxony was the worst of all the princes, but they all wanted more or less to be as like Louis XIV. as they could, and imitated him in his selfish vices and extravagances if they could do so in nothing else. They despised German as a vulgar language, and spoke hardly anything but French, while they made all the display they could, and as they were mostly very poor, this could only be done by getting everything they could out of their unhappy peasants, who were very rough, boorish, and uncared for. Nor had the cities by any means recovered from the effects of the Thirty-Years' War.

CHAPTER XL.

KARL VI., ... 1711-1740.

THE Archduke Karl was still at Barcelona when he heard the news of his brother's death, which gave him all the hereditary possessions of the House of Hapsburg. He sailed at once for Genoa, while Prince Eugene so dealt with the Electors that they chose Karl Emperor, and he was crowned at Frankfort, and afterwards as King of Hungary at Presburg.

But the crowns of the Empire and of Spain were not to be joined again by another Karl. The power of Marlborough's war-party was over with Queen Anne of England, and the Earl of Oxford thought it would be better to let Philip of France keep Spain, and that old Louis XIV. ought not to be pushed any further. Karl meant, however, **to fight on, and sent Eugene to England to try to per-**

suade Queen Anne to continue the war, but the Savoyard was not courtly enough to please her, and people in London were disappointed to see a little,

KARL VI.

dry, insignificant-looking elderly man instead of the hero they expected. He gained nothing by his visit but a diamond-hilted sword for himself, and the English and Dutch troops were withdrawn from his army.

Then he tried to stir up the Germans to force Louis XIV. into giving up all that France had seized during that long reign, but, say what he would, nobody moved, and at last Karl consented to make peace. He gave up all claim to Spain, but he kept the Netherlands, which had belonged to the Spanish line ever since the marriage of Philip the Handsome and Juana the Mad, and the fortresses of Breisach, Friburg, and Kehl were restored to Germany. The island of Sardinia was also given up to him, and Sicily was given to the Duke of Savoy, while the claim of the King of Prussia to Neufchatel in Switzerland was acknowledged. This peace, which finished the war of the Spanish succession, is called the Peace of Utrecht, and was signed in September, 1713.

Victor Amadeus of Savoy found Sicily too far from his dukedom, so he exchanged it with the Emperor for Sardinia, and took the title of King of the last-mentioned isle.

The Electors of Bavaria and Köln were pardoned and returned to their lands, and the next year another Elector became a King, when George of Brunswick, Elector of Hanover, obtained the crown of England through the Act of Settlement, which shut out the Roman Catholic heirs. It must have been a misfortune to Köln to have such an Archbishop as their Elector restored, for he had no notion of the duties of his office. Once, during his exile, he gave notice that he was going to preach in the Court Chapel at Versailles on the 1st of April, and when a large congregation had assembled he appeared in the pulpit, shouted out, "April fools all!" and ran away, to the sound of trumpets and kettle-drums.

His nephew, Karl Albrecht of Bavaria, and his wife lived disgraceful lives, given up to pleasure. They were great hunters, and the lady kept twelve dogs always close to her bedroom, and two in it, and she not only beat her dogs, but her courtiers with her own hand.

The Markgraf of Baden, Karl, who built Karlsruhe, was another byword for gross self-indulgence, and the most respectable court among the German princes was that of Friedrich Wilhelm II., King of Prussia. He was a rough, plain, religious man, but with the taste and manner of a drill-sergeant. He cared for nothing so much as his army, and for getting a set of giants for his guards; he carried on business with his ministers and generals sitting at a table, smoking their pipes over tankards of beer. He so hated French politeness and the vices which had come in with it, that he was perfectly brutal in his manners to his wife and daughters, and greatly misused his clever son Friedrich, who had a passion for everything French. When the young man tried to escape with his friend, Lieutenant Katt, they were seized, and treated as deserters. Katt was shot, and Friedrich forced to stand and see his friend's death, after which he had a long imprisonment, till, when his father forgave him, he was suddenly brought out and placed behind his mother's chair while she was playing at cards.

In the meantime, Prince Eugene was carrying on a great war with the Turks on the Hungarian frontier, where he was joined by all who wanted to see good service. He beat the Grand Vizier at Carlowitz, and then took Temeswar, and laid siege to Belgrade. The Turks came, 250,000 in number, to its relief, and encamped on the heights above, while Eugene lay ill of a fever in his tent. On the 1st of August, 1717, he was recovered enough to give them battle. He attacked them in the middle of the night, and gained a most splendid **victory**, which immediately gave him possession of

Belgrade, and he placed guards along the whole bank of the Danube to watch against the Turks.

Karl VI. had no son, and the great object of the latter half of his life was to cheat his nieces in favor of his daughters. He betrothed his daughters to the sons of the Duke of Lorraine, and obtained from the diet and from the powers of Europe consent to a Pragmatic Sanction, by which the eldest, Maria Theresa, was to succeed to all his hereditary states. To get the support of Saxony, Karl gave his support to Friedrich August II., who claimed the crown of Poland on his father's death, against Stanislas Lecksinsky. The daughter of Stanislas was wife to Louis the XV., and thus there was another war with France. Eugene, at seventy-one, took the command, and was hailed by the army with shouts of, "Our father," while Friedrich Wilhelm of Prussia saluted, saying, "I see my master." But there was not much to be done, the French took Philipsburg, and Eugene was recalled, and took leave of his army, and went back to Vienna, where he spent the last two years of his life in deeds of beneficence. He was so good a master that his servants grew old under him, and in the last year of his life the united ages of himself, his coachman, and two footmen amounted to 310. He now and then tried to give advice to Karl, but was not heeded, though he was missed and mourned when he died suddenly at seventy-three, in 1719.

He had been the only man in the Council of War who did not cheat, and the army, though counted at 120,000, was really only 40,000, and they were half-starved, half-clothed, and had useless weapons, so they were beaten in Italy by the French and Spaniards, and in Hungary by the Turks, and Karl had to make the best peace he could. It was a strange arrangement — Friedrich August of Saxony was to keep Poland, and Stanislas Lecksinsky was to have Lorraine, and leave it to his daughter, the French Queen. The real Duke Franz, husband to Maria Theresa, was to have Tuscany instead, and everybody again promised that she should have the Austrian dominions, and gave hopes that her husband should be chosen Emperor, he being descended from Karl the Great.

But faith, truth, and honesty were little heeded. Everybody preyed upon the Emperor, and the waste was beyond belief. Two hogsheads of Tokay wine were said to be used daily for dipping the bread on which the Empress's parrots were fed, twelve gallons of wine were supposed to be used every day for her possetts, and twelve barrels for her baths, while all the Austrian states were in a wretched state of want and misery, all because Karl was dull and unheeding. He died on the 12th of October, 1740, the last male heir of the House of Hapsburg.

CHAPTER XLI.

KARL VII................ 1740.

NOBODY cared for Karl VI.'s Pragmatic Sanction any more than he had cared for Joseph's Family Compact. No sooner was he dead than the husbands of the two daughters of Joseph put forward their claim; Marie Josepha had married Friedrich August of Saxony, King of Poland, and Maria Amalie, Karl, Elector of Bavaria, who was also descended from Ferdinand I.

Moreover, Friedrich II. of Prussia, who had that year succeeded his father, the old Corporal of Potsdam, was determined to use his fine army to get something for himself, so, only a month after the Emperor's death, he dashed into Silesia, and seized a number of towns. Then he wrote to Maria Theresa that he would support her claims and vote

Maria Theresa.

for her husband as Emperor if she would give up the province to him.

Marie Theresa was a beautiful and brave young woman of three-and-twenty, and would not submit to such treatment. She sent her army against the Prussians, and a battle was fought at Mollwitz, when Friedrich thought all was lost, and galloped off the field, saying to his staff—"Adieu, messieurs, I am the best mounted;" but when he saw them again, it was to find that, so far from being routed, they had gained a complete victory.

France and Spain joined Bavaria, Saxony, and Prussia against Maria Theresa, and at the diet at Frankfort in 1742, Karl of Bavaria was chosen Emperor, but without the vote of George II. of England, the Elector of Hanover, and the only ally of the brave young Queen. Karl invaded Austria, and August, Bohemia; Vienna was in danger, but Karl was jealous of the progress of the Saxons, and turned aside to secure Bohemia, which he mastered for a time. He was crowned at Prague, and set out to receive the Imperial crown at Frankfort.

Maria Theresa was driven from city to city, but she was resolved not to give up one jot of her inheritance. Her hope was in the Hungarians, and when she went to Presburg to be crowned, she appeared before the diet in robes of deep mourning for her father, but jewelled all over, and with the sacred crown of St. Stephen on her head, her fair hair flowing below in rich curls, the sword girded to her waist, and her little son Joseph in her arms. She made the diet a spirited speech in Latin, which was the state language in Hungary, which so stirred the hearts of the brave Magyar nobility, that they all waved their swords in the air, and cried out in one voice in Latin — "*Moriamur pro rege, Maria Theresia*" (Let us die for our King, Maria Theresa). Then she put on the royal breastplate, mounted a charger, and rode up the royal mount, defying the four corners of the world with her drawn sword in true kingly fashion.

Not only all the Hungarians, but their neighbors, the Croats and Transylvanians, mustered in her favor. The English raised money to equip them, and, in the meantime, her enemies were quarreling out of jealousy of one another; and Friedrich II. let her know that he would join her if she would give up the whole of Silesia to him.

On the very day on which Karl VII. was crowned at Aachen, Maria Theresa's brother-in-law, Charles V. of Lorraine, invaded Bavaria, and drove out the French army. However, he was soon after defeated by the Prussians at Czaslau, on the Bohemian border, and this loss brought the Queen of Hungary to consent to his terms, and give up Silesia to him, though with great grief and bitterness.

KARL VII.

She had also made peace with the King of Saxony, and had only Bavaria and France to fight with; but she had England on her side, and she hoped that she should conquer back again Lorraine, her husband's proper inheritance.

Prague was held by the French under Marshal Belleisle for the Emperor. It was closely blockaded by Prince Charles of Lorraine, who drove back the army coming to their help, and expected soon to have the whole French garrison in his hands; but it was the depth of winter, and the cold prevented his watching closely enough, so that Marshal Belleisle, with provisions for twelve days, made his way out at night with 14,000 men, only leaving behind him a small guard with the sick and wounded in the citadel. He reached Egra on the twelfth day, having lost only 100 men by attacks of the enemy, but 1200 by the frightful weather, so that the Bohemians found the roads dreadful to behold, for they were overspread with corpses, heaps of a hundred or more lying stiffened with frost all together. Still all the cannon and colors were saved, and when the guard in the citadel were summoned to surrender, their officer answered that unless he were allowed to march out with the honors of war, he should set fire to the four corners of the city, and perish in it.

He was therefore allowed to go free with his army, and Maria Theresa celebrated her conquest by a chariot race, as like those of the ancient Greeks as possible, considering that ladies drove in it, and the Queen and her sister were among the competitors.

On the 12th of May, 1743, Maria Theresa was crowned Queen of Bohemia, having thus gained all her hereditary dominions, which she ruled with great vigor and spirit, having set everything on a much better footing than had been in her father's time.

Her brother-in-law, Prince Charles, marched to punish the Emperor, and beat him and the French, so that Munich had to be deserted, and to obtain some kind of respite, he made a treaty with the Queen, engaging to remain neutral, and to renounce all his claims to the Austrian succession.

The war with France still went on, and the English and Austrian armies, with George the II. at their head, routed the French at Dettingen. The old days of Marlborough and Eugene seemed to be coming again, and Vienna was in transports of joy. The Queen was out on a water-party on the Danube when the news arrived, and the whole population poured out to meet her, and lined the banks for nine miles, shouting with ecstacy.

It was said of her that she was like the English

Elizabeth, in being able to make every man about her a hero; and, not contented with what she had recovered, she baffled George II.'s endeavors to make peace, being resolved to force Karl of Bavaria to resign the title of Emperor, and to conquer back Elsass and Lorraine. However, her attacks on these provinces did not prosper, and her other scheme was prevented by the death of the unfortunate Karl VII., who died early in 1745 from the shock of hearing, when already ill of the gout, of the defeat of the French in a skirmish. He advised his son, Maximilian Joseph, not to let himself, like him, be made a French tool, but to make his peace with Austria as soon as possible.

CHAPTER XLII.

FRANZ I., ... 1745–1765.

THERE was no difficulty made about electing Franz of Lorraine, the husband of Maria Theresa, Emperor on the death of Karl VII. The new Elector of Bavaria made his peace by giving him his vote, and Friedrich II. of Prussia acknowledged him. Maria Theresa was henceforth called the Empress Queen. She loved her husband heartily, but she let him have no authority in her own hereditary dominions, which she ruled in her own right, and an Emperor had by this time hardly any power over the princes of Germany, and was little more than a name.

The war in Germany was over, but that with France still lasted, with England still as the ally of Austria; but France had now a great general,

Marshal Saxe, a half-brother of the King of Saxony and he gained so many advantages that Maria Theresa and George II. at length consented to make peace with Louis XV. at Aachen, or, as the French call it, Aix-la-Chapelle, in 1748, and Europe had rest for eight years.

Meantime Friedrich II. was hard at work improving his country as well as his army, causing great works to be done in husbandry and in manufactures, and working up Prussia to be one of the foremost and most prosperous kingdoms in Europe, for he was a wonderfully clear and far-sighted man. Unhappily, the rude, harsh way in which his father had tried to force religion on him had given him a dislike to it, which made him think all piety folly. These were the days when the French were writing books full of sneers at all faith, and Friedrich, who despised everything German and admired everything French, never rested till he had brought the greatest unbeliever of them all, Voltaire, the witty writer of poetry, to his court at Potsdam. The guest was received with rapture, and Friedrich thought nothing too good for him; but the King and the poet were equally vain — Voltaire thought he could meddle with state affairs, and Friedrich fancied himself able to write poetry. They laughed at each other in private, and people carried the sayings of one to the other. Voltaire exclaimed, when Friedrich sent him some verses to correct—"Here is more of his dirty linen to wash;" and Friedrich was reported to have said he only wanted Voltaire till he could squeeze the orange and throw away the rind. Moreover, Voltaire gave himself great airs to the King's suite. Once, at dinner, he called a noble young page who was waiting a Pomeranian beast. When the youth was, shortly after, attending the Frenchman on a journey, he told the crowd that the little, thin, dry figure grinning and chattering in the carriage was the King's monkey, so when Voltaire tried to open the door they closed in to catch him, and the more he raged, the more monkey-like they thought him.

The two friends quarreled desperately, and Voltaire left Berlin in a passion, but was pursued and arrested because he had a poem of the King's in his boxes. However, he was soon set free, and afterwards they made up their quarrel, though without meeting.

Marie Theresa's heart was set on getting back Silesia, and most of the powers of Europe distrusted the King of Prussia. So she and her minister, Count Kaunitz, began to form alliances against

Friedrich. On his side he had made friends with England, and the Empress Queen laid aside her hatred to France, and agreed with Louis XV., the Empress Elizabeth of Russia, and the King of Saxony and Poland, to tame the pride of the House of Brandenburg.

Friedrich, finding out these alliances, sent to demand of Maria Theresa whether there was to be peace or war, and, on her answer, he began the Seven Years' War in 1756 by dashing into Saxony. He gained a victory at Lowositz, and pushed on to Dresden, where he sent his Scotch general, Marshal Keith, to demand the King's papers, where he knew he should find proofs of the league against him. The Queen—daughter to Joseph I.—refused to give them up, stood in front of the box, and sat upon it, only giving them up when she found the King would use violence. She was allowed to join her husband in Poland, where she died of grief for the misery of her country.

Then marching into Bohemia, Friedrich fought a dreadful battle with Charles of Lorraine, which lasted eleven hours. He gained the victory and besieged Prague, but was beaten at Kollin by the Austrian army who came to relieve it, and was so grieved at the disaster that he sat for hours silent

The Queen of Poland.

on a hollow tree, drawing figures in the sand with his stick.

He was forced to leave Bohemia, and in the meantime the Swedes and Russians were overrunning the Prussian provinces, and his English friends had been beaten at Hastenbeck by the French, and had left the way open into Prussia. Friedrich and his kingdom seemed as if they must be crushed among all these great powers. He had made up his mind to die rather than yield, and carried about with him a bottle of poison, though all the time he never ceased from his dry, sharp jokes. He was the most skillful captain in all Europe, and was able to save his country by a splendid victory over the French at Rossbach, and another over the Austrians at Leuthen. The next year, 1758, he beat the Russians at Zorndorf, but after that he suffered two defeats. He lost his faithful Scottish Marshal Keith at Zorndorf, and at Kunersdorf, when the battle was over, he had only 3000 men left out of 48,000, and had to sleep on straw in a hut, with three balls in his clothes. Dresden was taken by the Austrians, but the Russians had suffered so much in their victory that they had to retreat from Prussia.

The battle of Minden was fought to save

Hanover from the French by the English and Germans, and was a victory, though ill-managed. Friedrich was able to besiege Dresden, which he ruined by a cruel cannonade but could not take, for the Austrians were upon him again, took Berlin, and overran Prussia. Their General, Esterhazy, lodged in Potsdam itself, but he would not let it be plundered, and only took away one picture as a trophy. Meantime, Friedrich fought a frightful battle at Torgau in Saxony with Marshal Daun. He was struck down by a spent ball, and carried to the village church, where he lay on the floor writhing, and Marshal Zeithen fought on in the dark, thinking the battle lost, till morning light showed that the Austrians were driven away, and the field covered with heaps of slain.

Torgau was the last battle of the Seven Years' War. Everybody was worn out, and Maria Theresa found that though Prussia might seem overwhelmed for a moment, it always revived more fiercely than ever, and she consented to conferences being held at Hubertsberg. A treaty was made in 1763 by which Saxony went back to Angust III., and Silesia was left in the hands of Friedrich. Nothing had been gained by anyone in this horrible war, in which 640,000 men had died, and misery

Friedrich the Great and Zeithen.

unspeakable inflicted on the unhappy people of Saxony, Prussia, and Silesia.

Two years later, in 1775, Maria Theresa lost her husband, the Emperor Franz I., a good man, whom she loved devotedly, and called her heart's joy. She almost broke her heart when he died, she let no one sew his shroud but herself, and for the rest of her life used to spend many hours in praying by his coffin in the vault of the chapel of her palace at Vienna.

CHAPTER XLIII.

JOSEPH II. . . . . 1765–1790.

THE eldest of the many sons of Franz I. and Maria Theresa was elected Emperor, but his mother remained sovereign of her hereditary states, and the title of Emperor conveyed hardly any power. Germany was a collection of states, some large, but mostly very small. Prussia and Saxony, Bavaria and Wurtemburg, were large and powerful, but there were many like dukedoms and principalities, not so large as an English county, and these, like the free towns, belonged indeed to the Empire, but were no more ruled by the Emperor than were France or England.

August III. of Saxony died soon after his return from Dresden, and the crown of Poland was given to a noble named Stanislas Poniatowsky, whom the Empress Catherine of Russia forced the Poles to elect. Prussia meantime was recovering from its misfortunes under Friedrich II., whose wonderful skill in this terrible war had earned him the name of the Great. He helped the people who had suffered most with gifts of money and corn, he drained marshes, opened canals, and wonderfully improved the country. He did all this by taxes on salt, coffee, and tobacco, at which people grumbled a good deal, but he never punished any one for this, saying his people might talk as much as they pleased if they would only obey. Once when he found a crowd staring at a caricature of himself sitting on the ground with a coffee-mill between his legs, and the label, "Old Fritz, the coffee-grinder," he laughed at it, and had it pasted lower down on the wall that the people might see it better. He was very just even where his own plans were concerned, and left a windmill standing, an eye-sore to his favorite palace of Sans Souci, because the miller would not part with it. He built churches for both Protestants and Roman Catholics, but he had no fixed faith himself, and encouraged all kinds of bold questionings around him.

Young Joseph II. much admired him, and longed to bring in his reforms to Austria, but the Empress Queen would not hear of them. When her son wanted to pull down the walls that shut in Vienna, she said, "I am an old woman. I can almost remember Vienna besieged by the Turks. I have twice seen it almost the frontier of my dominions. Let Joseph do as he pleases when I am dead. While I live, Vienna shall not be dismantled."

Joseph, in his eagerness to copy the King of Prussia, went to visit him, under the name of Count Falkenstein, and the two were so delighted with one another that the Emperor always spoke of Friedrich as "the King, my master," and the King hung his rooms at Sans Souci with portraits of Joseph as "a young man of whom he could not see enough."

Joseph's head was already full of Friedrich's free-thinking notions, as well as of his able plans for his country, and he was now persuaded into a wicked scheme, contrived by Friedrich and by Catherine of Russia, who was likewise an unbeliever, namely, that the three powers — Russia, Austria, and Prussia, should seize on the unfortunate country of Poland, and divide it between them. It had always been badly governed; the kings were elective, and never had power enough to keep order, and the nobles were always fighting;

Maria Theresa and Kaunitz.

but that did not make the ruin of it less a wicked act on the part of the three nobles, and so thought the Empress Queen, who wrote that she had not been so unhappy even when she had hardly a city in which to lay her head, but Friedrich only laughed, and said, "I would as soon write the Jewish history in madrigals as make three sovereigns agree, especially when two are women."

She was old now, and, in spite of all she could say and write, her son and Kaunitz had their way, the Poles were too quarrelsome and broken into parties to make much resistance, and the plan was carried out, though not all at once.

In 1777 died Maximilian, Elector of Bavaria. Karl Theodoc of the Rhine was the right heir, but Joseph set up an unjust claim to two-thirds of it through one of his ancestresses, in spite of his mother, and frightened the Elector into yielding. However, Friedrich took up the cause, and marched into Bohemia, saying he was only come to teach a young gentleman his military exercise, and he managed so cleverly to avoid a battle that this was called the potato war, because the men did little but roast potatoes at their watch-fires. Maria Theresa wrote to Friedrich that she could not bear that they should begin again to tear one another's grey hairs, at which Joseph was very angry, but at last peace was made at Teschen, to her great delight.

After this, Joseph set out to make a visit to the Russian Empress. His favorite way of traveling was to ride on before his suite, pretending to be a courier sent on to order horses, dine on a sausage and some beer, and ride on as soon as the carriages came in sight. Thus he found out how to do many kind acts. Once he offered to stand godfather to a child newly born in a poor hut, and amazed the parents by coming to the christening in full state as Emperor; and another evening he supped with an officer with a poor pension, who had ten children of his own, but had adopted an orphan besides. Soon after came a letter from the Emperor, endowing each of the eleven with two hundred florins a-year.

Joseph came home in 1780, just as his mother was dying, leaving nine survivors out of her sixteen children. She had been a good woman, a pious and upright queen, and she was greatly loved by her people, whom she had heartily loved and worked for. Her death left Joseph free to try to follow his favorite Friedrich's example, and to sweep away all that he thought worn-out and use-

Joseph II Holding the Plough.

less. So would not go to be crowned in **Hungary** because he would not swear to obey the old constitution, and he carried off the crown of St. Stephen to Vienna. Love of his mother prevented a rebellion, but there was great discontent at the changes he made.

In all his dominions he made changes. He forbade his clergy to appeal to the Pope, he altered bishoprics, broke up three hundred convents, leaving only those that were schools, prevented pilgrimages, and removed images from the churches. The Pope, Pius VI., came to Vienna to plead with him, but the Emperor treated him with cold civility, and would not let the Austrian clergy visit him, even walling up the back door of his house lest they should get in privately.

Joseph wanted to exchange the Netherlands for the duchy of Bavaria, but Friedrich the Great induced all the other German powers to make a league against any change in the Empire, and he had to give way. It was the last work of Friedrich, who was so ill that he could neither ride, walk, nor lie down, though he still attended to business, listened to the books of the day, and played with his dogs, the beings he seemed to love best. He even desired to be buried among them in his garden when he died in 1786, and was succeeded by his nephew, Friedrich Wilhelm II., having made his little kingdom a great power.

Joseph had not strength or skill to succeed in an old country as he had done in a new one. Everyone was in a state of grief and anger at the changes, and he declared his heart must be of stone not to break when he found that, while he meant to do good, he had only done harm, and made enemies of his mother's faithful people. He tried to help the Russian Empress to conquer the Turks, hoping to get a share for himself, but he lost many men in the marshes on the Danube from illness and in skirmishes, and he caught a fever himself, and came home to Vienna ill, and grieved at the bad news which came in from all sides. "My epitaph should be — 'Here lies a monarch who, with the best intentions, never carried out a single plan,'" he said. And he soon died, broken-hearted, in his 49th year, on the 20th of February, 1790.

CHAPTER XLIV.

LEOPOLD II................1790-1792.

LEOPOLD, the next brother to Joseph, had received the duchy of Tuscany on his father's death, and had ruled there twenty-five years. He came to the crown in very dangerous times, amid the troubles that had darkened the last days of Joseph.

Hungary had revolted, saying Joseph had broken all their laws, and that, as the direct male line of Hapsburg had failed, they had the right of choosing their King. Moreover, the Netherlands had been angry at the interference of Joseph with their old laws, and had revolted, and set up a republic on their own account, and there was a terrible example close at hand in France of the dangers that might beset kings who had tried their people's patience too long. Leopold's youngest sister, Marie

Antoinette, was, with her husband, Louis XVI., threatened daily by the mob of Paris, while the National Assembly were changing all the laws and institutions, and viewed the King and Queen as their greatest enemies, hating her especially as an Austrian, as they considered the Hapsburgs as the great foes of France. She was like a prisoner in her own palace, while Germany, like all the countries, was fast filling with emigrant nobles, who fled from the savage violence of the people, who rose to revenge the long course of oppression they had suffered.

Germany being the easiest country to reach, a much lower and worse stamp of emigrants went thither than those who came to England. There they behaved well, and made themselves respected as well as pitied, but in Germany many lived low, dissipated lives, and increased the taste the Germans had for French manners and language, and, unfortunately, for French fashions and vices.

Leopold could do nothing to help his sister, for Friedrich Wilhelm III. of Prussia, a vicious and selfish man, hoping to rise on the ruins of the House of Austria, encouraged all the disturbances in the Austrian dominions, and let the discontented Hungarian nobles hold meetings at Berlin. Moreover, the war with Turkey which Joseph had begun was still going on.

The Austrians took the city of Orsova, but after trying to besiege Widdin, they were obliged to make a truce with the Turks, because the Prussian King had taken up arms against them, and had a great army in Silesia, with which he threatened to invade the Austrian province of Gallicia, and as he still had in his army many of the old generals of Friedrich the Great, he thought himself able to do everything. However, the English and Dutch came forward, and made peace between Austria and Prussia, and Prussia then mediated between Austria and Turkey.

After this, the King of Prussia voted for Leopold's election as Emperor, and he was crowned at Frankfort. At the same time he quieted his Austrian subjects by undoing some of the changes to which they had most objected, and tried to govern as much as possible in his mother's spirit, which, though it seemed to the new way of thinking narrow and unenlightened, was kind and fatherly, and suited the loyal Austrians and Tyrolese.

He had more trouble with Hungary, which was always turbulent, and which had been completely unsettled by Joseph's reforms and the resistance to them, and the nobles sent him a set of demands which he would not grant, only promising to govern Hungary as his grandfather and mother had done. They were obliged to be satisfied, and he sent the crown of St. Stephen to Presburg, and came thither himself, with his five sons, for his coronation. The Hungarians welcomed him warmly, and they chose his fourth son, Leopold, to act as their Palatine, and to place the crown upon his father's head.

He then prepared to teach the Netherlands to submit to him, and entered the country. The States were of various minds as to what they wanted, their leaders were quarreling, and they ended by yielding to him one by one, but not without leaving a great deal of discontent, which was much increased by all that was passing in France.

Leopold was free now to do something for his sister and her husband, and he allied himself with Prussia and Spain, preparing armies to march upon France, while the emigrant nobles eagerly enlisted. He sent messages to the King and Queen of France that they had better wait patiently till he could rescue them, and try to win back their people's hearts, but that he meant to assist them not by words but deeds. In truth, the invasion he intended was the very worst thing for poor Louis and Marie Antoinette, for it only made the people

LEOPOLD II.

more furious with them, thinking them guilty of bringing in foreign enemies to crush the freedom newly won. Knowing this, the King and Queen tried to escape, but were seized and brought back again, amid hooting and all kinds of ill-usage.

Moreover, Leopold found it less easy to begin a war with the French than he had expected. The English would not take up arms, and his ministers said that he would only lose the Netherlands, which the French coveted above all things, and that to be friends with them would make them treat his sister better. So he acknowledged their new constitution, and let their Ambassodor at Vienna set up his tri-colored flag.

But there was no use in trying to make peace, for the French looked on all monarchs as mere wolves, and besides, they wanted to have the emigrants driven from Germany, and to seize the Netherlands. So war was decided on, but just before it began Leopold fell ill, and died in his 45th year, in February, 1792. His Empress, Marie Louisa of Spain, died of grief three months later. Like his mother, he had a family of sixteen children, of whom all but two lived to grow up. The second son, the Archduke Karl, became a great general. Leopold had tried to hold things together, but everything in Germany was in a rotten state, and he was happy in dying before the troubles came to a head.

CHAPTER XLV.

FRANZ II., ... 1792.

FRANZ II. succeeded his father just as the war had begun, and the Prussians, under Ferdinand, Duke of Brunswick, and accompanied by the King himself, were crossing the Rhine, accompanied by a large force of French emigrants, who burned to rescue their King and Queen. Several places were taken, but instead of pushing on at once, before Paris was prepared, the Duke of Brunswick put forth a proclamation, calling on the French to return to their duty, and threatening not to leave one stone of Paris on another if a hair on the head of any of the royal family was touched.

This put the whole French nation in a fury; they flocked to join the army, and, ill-fed and half-trained though they were, they beat the Prussians at **Valmy,** and drove them beyond the Rhine, and at the same time the Paris mob, in their fright and anger, massacred all the royalists in the prisons for fear they should join their friends outside.

The Austrian army had likewise entered France, but was entirely defeated at Jemappes, and had to retreat before the French. The Netherlands, where Austrian rule was hated, immediately rose and made themselves into a Republic, under the protection of France, and at Paris the captive king was put to trial as a traitor who had called in the foreign enemy, and was executed.

All Europe was indignant, and the French declared war on all the states at once, with a fierce energy that was too much for the old-fashioned habits of the Germans and Austrians, who were beaten again and again. Franz himself joined the army in the Netherlands, and for a time gained the advantage, but was beaten by General Pichegru at Tournay, and was again defeated at Fleurus; so that he had to fall back while the French entered Holland, and moulded the Republic to their own fashion.

Prussia was called off from the war by a great rising in its ill-gotten possession, Poland led on by a gallant noble named Kosciusko, who hoped to win freedom for his country. Friedrich Wilhelm was obliged to call on Russia to help him to put down the revolt, and the three robbers, Prussia, Austria, and Russia, quarrelled over the plunder, so that Prussia would no longer hold to the alliance with Austria, but made a seperate peace with France in 1795.

Then the French army, under Bonaparte, crossed the Alps, and attacked the Austrian power in Italy, where they gained wonderful successes. The Archduke Karl was fighting gallantly with the other French troops in Germany, but the quick movements of the young generals were a great deal too perplexing to the old German soldiers, who were used to go by the old rules of 100 years ago, and the French drove them back everywhere. The army of Italy was driving the Austrians back into their own country, though on every height in the Tyrol stood the brave chamois hunters, marking the invaders down with their guns; but there was no stopping Bonaparte, and he came out on the northern slope, so that Vienna felt how wise Maria Theresa had been in not letting the fortifications be taken down. The Emperor sent his little children away into Hungary, and the city made ready for a siege.

But the army on the Rhine could not fight its

way across to join Bonaparte's army, and he could get no more men without going himself to France, so he took upon himself to make peace, and a treaty was made at Campo Formio, by which Austria gave up the Netherlands and the North of Italy, and was to have in return the old city of Venice, which the French seized in time of peace, and made over to Franz. He was not ashamed to accept it though it had never belonged to Austria, not even to the German Empire.

There was a little calm in Europe while Bonaparte went off on his expedition to Egypt. During this time Friedrich Wilhelm II. of Prussia died, in 1797, having spent all the treasure his two predecessors had laid up, and leaving his country in a much worse state than that in which he had received it. His successor, Friedrich Wilhelm III., was personally a much better man, and had a most excellent wife, Louise of Mecklenburg-Strelitz, but he was a weak man, and let his father's old ministry go on with the same mean and shabby policy as before.

The French kept few of their promises in the treaty, and the Austrians, thinking their best troops and most terrible captain would be lost in Egypt, **believed that this** would be the time **to win back** what had been lost to them, and again joined England and Russia in declaring war upon France. The Russian army came through Austria into Italy, and nearly conquered back Lombardy and Tuscany, but the Czar declared that everybody should have their own again, and Franz did not choose to give up Venice, besides which they were always ready to dispute about Poland. However, the Archduke Karl was successful on the Rhine, and things went hopefully till Bonaparte suddenly came home from Egypt, hurried to Italy, and in the great battle of Marengo so entirely beat the Austrian General Melas that the French gained back all they had lost.

In Germany the Archduke Johann was trying to defend Bavaria against the French, under Moreau, and on the 1st of December, 1800, gained a little advantage over him when between the Rivers Inn and Iser. Setting out in the middle of the night, Johann marched through the forest of Hohenlinden, in the midst of a heavy snowstorm, hoping to surprise the French in their camp; but the enemy were up and elert, and there was a dreadful battle, fought in the midst of such thick snow that the soldiers could not see one another, only the flash of the muskets on either side, and 7000 fell on each side.

> "Few, few shall part, where many meet!
> The snow shall be their winding-sheet.
> And every turf beneath their feet
> Shall be a soldier's sepulchre.„

Hohenlinden ended in the utter defeat of the Archduke, and Franz was again forced to make peace, at Luneville, giving up to France all the lands beyond the Rhine, and acknowledging the Republics that had been formed out of the states of the Empire and its own lands. The princes who thus lost their lands received property and cities that used to be free in Germany. Forty-eight cities were thus stripped of their freedom, and only Lubeck, Hamburg, Bremen, Frankfurt, and Nuremberg remained free.

In these evil times there were greater men in Germany in literature than at any other time The ablest poet of them all was Goëthe, who lived at the little town of Weimar, admired by the Duke, and making a world of poetry for himself, in which he was so wrapped up that he cared nothing at all for the changes and misfortunes of his country.

CHAPTER XLVI.

FRANZ II., ... 1804-1806.

AFTER the peace or Luneville, Napoleon Bonaparte made himself Emperor of the French, and Franz II. congratulated him; but it was not long possible to avoid war with such a neighbor. The Emperor was very much affronted by all the North of Italy, which had been made into little Republics under French protection, being attached to the new Empire, as if it had belonged to France. Moreover, because Hanover belonged to George III. of England, with whom France was at war, it was seized by French troops, but the German princes were some of them afraid of Napoleon, some dazzled by his glory, and it was not easy to move them against him. When Franz resolved to renew the war, and called the princes together, the Prussians were bribed by Napoleon by being allowed a share of Hanover, and the Elector of Bavaria desired leave to wait till his son, who was traveling in France, should be safe out of the enemy's country. Franz was angered at this, and sent General Mack to occupy Bavaria; and the Duke of Wurtemburg and Markgraf of Baden, who were already admirers of Napoleon, were so angered at this step that they likewise went over to the French interest. Napoleon hurried into Bavaria with his troops so suddenly that Mack, who was a dull heavy man, was quiet stupefied, and let himself be cut off from Vienna and shut into Ulm, where he soon yielded to the enemy, with his army of 30,000 men.

By this time the Czar Alexander of Russia was coming to the help of Austria. Franz went to Presburg to meet him, and left Vienna undefended, so that it fell into the hands of the French, and Napoleon lodged in Maria Theresa's palace at Schönbrunn.

The Austrians and Russians, however were marching on him, and at Austerlitz, on the 2nd of December, 1805, there was a great battle, in which they were so totally defeated that Franz lost heart, and though his brothers were coming up with large armies, and the Russians would not have deserted him, he made another peace with France at Pres-

Napoleon and Franz II.

burg, giving up Venice to the new kingdom of Italy, and his own faithful dukedom of the Tyrol to Bavaria, while the Elector of Bavaria and Duke of Wurtemburg were made independent kings, and Cleves and Berg were made into a Grand Duchy for Napoleon's brother-in-law, General Joachim Murat.

The German princes were persuaded to form themselves into what was called the Confederation of the Rhine, with the Kings of Bavaria and Wurtemburg at its head, and the French Empire for their so-called protector, detaching themselves entirely from the great old Holy Roman Empire, which reckoned back through Karl the Great to Cæsar Augustus. The old Germanic League, with its Electoral college and its Diets, and the Kaisar at the head of all, was entirely broken up, and Franz II. resigned its crown on the 6th of August, 1806. He still remained King of Hungary and Bohemia and Archduke of Austria, and it would have been in better taste so to have called himself; but he would not give up the title of Emperor, though that really meant the commander of princes, and so he termed himself Hereditary Emperor of Austria.

Prussia was much disturbed at the Germanic Confederation, and Napoleon wanted to break down the power of that little soldierly kingdom, so though it had been neutral during the war, he picked a quarrel with it by threathening to give Hanover back to the King of England, and by most unworthy slanders of the Queen of Prussia, Louise of Mecklenburg. She was a good and lovely woman, and everybody loved her, but she was known to have been much grieved at the unmanly way in which her country had stood still all this time, and therefore he hated and maligned her. If she had been able to stir up her husband before the battle of Austerlitz, it might have been of some use, but it was too late when, in 1806, he called on Napoleon to remove his armies from Germany. The country was so delighted that the young men sharpened their swords on the steps at the door of the French ambassador at Berlin. The Russian Emperor Alexander came to promise his support, and joined hands with the Queen at midnight over the tomb of Friedrich the Great to confirm the alliance, then went back to send the aid he promised. Prussia would have done wisely to wait for it, but the whole nation rose eagerly in arms, and, uniting with Saxony and Hesse, raised an army of 150,000 men, who were placed under the Duke of Brunswick, now seventy-two years of age.

They had risen too late to act with Austria, too soon to act with Russia, and Napoleon was upon them at once, meeting them in Saxony, where he forced the passage of the Saale, killing the brave young Prince Ludwig of Prussia, the King's brother, on the bridge.

On the 14th of October, 1806, a dreadful battle was fought at Jena, where the Prussians were ill-commanded, and their valor only led to the slaughter of large numbers. Poor Queen Louise was in her carriage within sound of the guns, and had to drive away without knowing her husband's fate. He was safe, but the Duke of Brunswick was mortally wounded, and 20,000 men lay dead on the field. General Blucher with the survivors, roamed about for three weeks and fought a sharp battle at Lubeck, but had to surrender.

The King and Queen fled to Konigsberg, while the French entered Berlin, and Napoleon sent off all the relics of the great Friedrich as trophies to Paris. August III. of Saxony joined the Germanic Confederation, and was forgiven, but Napoleon punished the others who had dared to stand out against him with brutal harshness. He would not let the wounded old Duke of Brunswick lie down to die in peace, but said he might go to England,

and hunted him as far as Altona, where he died. In memory of him his son raised a regiment entirely dressed in mourning, with a skull and cross-bones as their badge, and these Black Brunswickers made it their business to fight wherever the French could be attacked.

The French were going to push on into Polish Prussia, when Alexander of Russia came down with his army, and fought two terrible battles at Eylau and Friedland, in which, though he was scarcely worsted, he was forced to retreat and Konigsburg was left open to the enemy, so that Friedrich Wilhelm and Louise had to retreat to Memel.

CHAPTER XLVII.

FRENCH CONQUESTS.

INTERREGNUM., ... 1807–1815.

AFTER the two doubful battles, Russia deserted the cause of Prussia. Alexander and Napoleon made peace at Tilsit, and sent for the King of Prussia to hear what they would leave to him. The Queen came with him, hoping to obtain better terms, but Napoleon treated her with rude scorn, and said that he had been like waxed cloth to rain. Once, when he offered her a rose, she said, " Yes, but with Magdeburg." "It is I who give, you who take," said Bonaparte roughly. He took away from Prussia all the lands on the Elbe and the Rhine, and these, with Brunswick, Hesse, Cassel, and part of Hanover, were made into a new kingdom of Westphalia for his brother Jerome. Polish Prussia was given to the King of Saxony, Dantzic made a free town, and only Prussia itself left to the King on condition that he should only keep an army of 42,000 men. The Queen pined away under grief and shame for her country's loss, and died two years later, leaving her people's hearts burning against the French tyranny, and longing to throw off the yoke. Though allowed to keep only such a small army on foot, it was made a means of training the whole nation to arms, for every man in turn served in it for a certain time, and then returned to his home while his place was taken by another.

The Emperor Franz took up arms again in 1809, sending his brother Karl to invade Bavaria; but this war turned out worse than ever for Austria. Karl was beaten at Eckmuhl; and though he won the victory of Aspern, he was driven across the Danube, and had another defeat at Wagram, so close to Vienna that the battle was watched from the walls. Again peace had to be made, and all the southern parts of the Austrian dominions had to be given up, while, greatest humiliation of all, Franz actually was forced to give his young daughter Marie Louise to be the wife of this Corsican soldier, though he was married to Josephine de la Pagerie, whom he divorced.

The Tyrol had been yielded to Bavaria, but the brave peasants, who were mostly farmers and huntsmen, rose on behalf of their Emperor, under an inn-keeper named Andreas Hofer, who led them most gallantly against the French and Bavarian troops, till an overwhelming force was sent against them, and they were crushed. Hofer was made prisoner, and shot at Mantua.

Germany had fallen to the very lowest point, and the French proved most rude and harsh masters. Any sign of disaffection was punished by death, and the young men were called away from their homes to serve in the Grand Army which Napoleon was raising to invade Russia; but all the time there was a preparation going on for shaking themselves free, and all over the German states men belonged to the *Tugendbund*, or bond of virtue, which was secretly vowed to free the land once more. Napoleon marched through Prussia, on his expedition to Moscow, in the summer of 1812. In the winter the miserable remnant of his Grand Army came straggling back, broken, starved, and wretched; and though for very pity the Prussians housed and fed them, it was with the glad certainty that the time of freedom was come. The Emperor Alexander followed with his victorious army, and

Friedrich Wilhelm met him at Breslau, shedding tears of joy. "Courage, brother, these are the last tears Napoleon shall draw from you."

Gebhard Blucher was the chief Prussian general. He was nicknamed Marshal Forwards, because that was always his cry, and Napoleon said he was like a bull rushing on danger with his eyes shut. All North Germany rose except the King of Saxony, who remained faithful to the alliance with France. Germans, Swedes, and Prussians together fought a battle at Lützen with the French, round the stone which marked where Gustaf Adolf had fallen, but neither this nor the ensuing battle of Bautzen ended well for them, and the poor city of Hamburg was horribly maltreated by the French General Davoust.

The Emperor of Austria sent his minister, Clemens Metternich, to tell Napoleon that he must join the rest of Germany against him. Napoleon was so angry that he asked what England had paid Austria for deserting him. Metternich scorned to answer, and they walked up and down the room on opposite sides for some time in silence. However, Franz sent his troops, under Prince Schwartzenberg, to join the other allies, and there was a battle

Metternich and Napoleon

at Leipsic, lasting three days, from the 16th to the 18th October, 1813, in which, after terrible slaughter, the Allies gained a complete victory. The rest of Germany rose and expelled the French, and the Allies were able the next winter to push on into France itself — the Prussians, with Blucher, over the Rhine; the Austrians, under Swartzenberg, through Switzerland. They were beaten singly in many battles, but the Swedes, Russians, and English were all advancing on different sides, and even Napoleon could not make head against five nations at once.

So they closed in on Paris, in April, 1814, and the Emperors of Russia and Austria and the King of Prussia all met there, and encamped their troops in the Champs Elysees and on the Boulevards. They saw Louis XVIII. placed on the throne by the French, and then made a visit to England, where Blucher was received with such enthusiasm that people pulled hairs out of his horse's tail as relics.

Napoleon was exiled to Elba, and a Congress met at Vienna to consider how the boundaries of the European states should be restored, after the great overthrow of them all; but in the midst of the consultations came the tidings that the prisoner had escaped, that the French army had welcomed him, and that Louis the XVIII. had again fled. Again the armies were mustered to march upon him, but only the Prussian was ready to join with the English in the Netherlands, where in June a succession of battles was fought, ending in the crowning victory of Waterloo on the 18th of June. Again the Allies occupied Paris, and Napoleon became a prisoner in the distant Atlantic island where he died. His wife, Marie Louise, had returned to her father with her little son, who died in early youth at Vienna. The Congress returned to its task at Vienna. The German Empire was not restored, and Electors and Imperial chambers were no more. There was only a great confederation of thirty-nine states, including the empire of Austria, the kingdoms of Prussia, Saxony, Hanover, and Wurtemburg, with Grand Duchies and principalities, and four free towns, Lubeck, Bremen, Hamburg, and Frankfort. They were not to make war on each other, nor with other nations, without each other's consent, and the Emperor was their president. Austria, however, only belonged to it for her German lands, not for the Italian states

The Allies Entering Paris.

which were given to her, though she gave up the Netherlands to be joined with Holland in one kingdom. The fortresses of Luxemburg, Mainz, and Landau were to belong to the whole Confederation, and be garrisoned by their troops.

CHAPTER XLVIII.

INTERREGNUM........ .... 1815–1835.

THERE was a time of rest after the twenty-five years of war, while the world recovered from the ruin it had caused; but the Congress of Vienna had so left matters that there was sure to be another disturbance soon. Prince Matternich, who managed everything for Franz II., kept all down with a firm hand, and nothing was so much shunned and dreaded by kings and their ministers as giving any power to the people.

Franz was a weak, dull man himself, kindly in his ways to those about him, and his own Austrians, among whom he walked about in an easy, friendly way, loved him; but in Italy there was great dislike to the Austrian power. The officers and soldiers who were quartered in the Italian cities were rough and insolent, and there were secret societies formed among the Italians for shaking off the yoke and freeing themselves. The men of this society were called Carbonari; but the time was not ripe for their plans— they were put down, and Franz kept the chief of them for many years in solitary confinement. Two of them Silvio Pellico and Alexandre Andryane, have written interesting histories of their imprisonment.

Franz died in 1835, and his son Ferdinand IV. was still more weak and dull, but Metternich still managed everything. Hanover was disjoined from England in 1837, as the succession was in the male line, and it was inherited on the death of William IV. by his brother Ernst August. In Prussia, Friedrich Wilhelm III. was succeeded in 1840 by his son fourth of the name, a good man, anxious to do right, but timid and weak, and rather confused between his notions of a king's power and his goodwill to his subjects. All this time the Germans were improving much in the learning, the art, the manufactures, and all that had been hindered before by the constant wars in which they lived. The northern Germans had the chief thinkers and writers; the southern had the greatest taste in art. King Ludwig I. of Bavaria set himself to encourage architects, sculptors, and painters, and made his city of Munich a wonderful place for beauty of all sorts, with splendid galleries of Pictures, ancient and modern. But he was a pleasure-loving man, who could not make himself respected, and in his old age he fell under the influence of a bad woman named Lola Montes, and his vice and folly shocked his people so much that he had to resign in favor of his son Maximilian. Prince Metternich had always hoped to hold things together as long as he lived in the old manner, and he used to say, "After me the deluge." But the deluge he meant came in his time.

When Pope Pius IX. began to reign at Rome, in 1846, he showed a wish to give more freedom to the people, and this filled all Italy with hope, and caused plans to be made for throwing over their harsh masters. There was a revolution in France in 1847, when King Louis Philippe was driven away, and the Germans began likewise to rise, especially the young students, whose heads were full of schemes of free government. Vienna was not safe for the Emperor or his minister. Ferdinand went to Innspruck, in his faithful Tyrol, and Metternich fled to England. In Berlin there was a great rising, and some fights between the people and the soldiers, till the King promised to grant the changes in the government that were wanted.

The German states all wanted to be one, and act together again, and send representatives to hold a great meeting at Frankfort to try to arrange some general plan. They chose the Archduke Johann of Austria to be the head of a new government which was to take them all in, but the plan turned out too clumsy to work, and there was nothing but confusion, while things were still worse in the Austrian dominions. Vienna was in an uproar, which the Emperor could not put down, and the Hungarians had risen, declaring that they had been unfairly treated, and wanted their rights. The wife of the Austrian governor, Princess Pauline Windischgratz, daughter of the general Schwartzenberg, was standing at a window above the street at Pesth when she was shot dead, and Count Lomburg was murdered. The chief Hungarian leader, who was named Kossuth, demanded that the Magyars, the old name by which his people called themselves, should be made free of all German power; he seized the capital and St. Stephen's crown, and when the Austrian troops were ordered to march against him, a number of the soldiers refused to leave Vienna or march against patriots.

Some of the troops remained faithful, but many young students joined the mutineers, and there was a great fight, in which the loyal troops were beaten, and then a number of men rushed upon the minister who had given orders to march into Hungary, and killed him. The Emperor, whose health was weak, and whose hand was not strong enough to rule in such times, went to his palace at Almutz, grieved and overwhelmed at such treatment from the Viennese, among whom he had been wont to walk about without any state, and to talk on the most kindly terms, like all his forefathers since Maria Theresa, meeting every one freely on the Prader, the beautiful public garden of Vienna.

The rebels shut themselves up in Vienna, and made ready for a siege, but the main body of the Austrians, and especially the Tyrolese, were still loyal, and troops came in numbers to Ferdinand's aid. After five days of much fighting and bloodshed the city was surrendered. Some of the rebel leaders fled; the others were taken and shot. Then Ferdinand, feeling quite unequal to reign in such stormy times, called together a family council of his brothers and uncles, and ended by giving up his crowns to his nephew, Franz Joseph, a fine young man of eighteen, on the 1st of December, 1848.

In the meantime the Germans at Frankfort wanted to have a real emperor again, and begged Friedrich Wilhelm of Prussia to accept the Imperial crown, and call himself Kaisar der Deutschern, or of the Germans; but after considering the matter, he decided that they were not giving him power enough to be of any use, and that it was wiser not to be only a name and shadow, so he refused, and all their schemes came to nothing. There were disturbances in Bavaria, Saxony, and Baden, but the Prussians helped to put them down, and North Germany was at peace again by the July of 1848.

CHAPTER XLIX.

INTERREGNUM............1848.

THE young Emperor, Franz Joseph, had a great deal on his hands, but ere long Austria and all his German states had returned to obedience.

In Italy the whole country had risen. The Austrian Marshal Radetsky had been driven out of Milan, and Colonel Marinovitch had been murdered at Venice; the Duke of Modena had fled, the Pope and the Romans were on the Liberal party, and the King of Sardinia, Carlo Alberto, had declared war against Austria, and invited all the other states to join under him to turn the foreigners out of Italy. But they did not trust him, and were afraid of his getting too much power over them. Besides, the Italians talked much better than they fought, and Carlo Alberto was not much of a general, so

Radetsky beat him at Custoza, came into Milan again, and then of course his troops were harsher than ever towards the Italians who had risen against them.

The Pope Pius IX., was afraid of fighting with the Austrians, and the Romans were so furious at his trying to draw back that they murdered his minister, Count Rossi, and this so much terrified the Pope that he disguised himself like a priest, and fled away on the box of a carriage to Gaeta, while the Romans set up a Republic. But none of the Italians could stand against the well-trained Austrian armies; so Radetsky defeated Carlo Alberto again at Novara, crushing his spirit so completely that he gave up his crown to his son Victor Emanuel, and died four months later of a broken heart. Then Radetsky laid siege to Venice, which held out bravely for four months, but it was taken at last, and the French at the same time restored the Papal government at Rome, so that Italy was very nearly in its former state; but there was more and more distrust on the Austrian side, and hatred on the Italian.

In the meantime the Hungarians had declared themselves independent of Austria, elected a Diet, and put Kossuth at the head. Franz Joseph could not subdue them, and asked the help of the Emperor Nicholas of Russia. The united Austrian and Russian armies defeated the Magyars, and put down the insurrection. The leaders escaped to Turkey, and Kossuth came to England, and afterwards went to live in America.

Still things in Germany were not in a state that could last, and there was much restlessness everywhere. In 1859 the Italians, having learned a lesson by their former failure, united again, and this time under the King of Sardinia, with the help of Napoleon III., Emperor of the French. The Austrian forces were beaten at Magenta, and then at Solferino; but afterwards Franz Joseph met Napoleon at Villa Franca, and persuaded him to forsake Victor Emanuel, and favor the setting up of a Confederation of all the little Italian states, instead of making them one strong kingdom; but **the** Sardinian king would not consent to **this**, and **the** people of the Tuscan and Lombardy dukedoms insisted on being made part of his kingdom. So they were given to him, and all Lombardy as far as the Mincio, but only on condition that he should give up to the French his own old dukedom of **Savoy. Seven years later, in 1866, Venice turned** out the Austrians, who had so unjustly been placed there by the first Napoleon, and a war began for freedom.

But Franz Joseph had another war on his hands by that time. The gentle undecided Friedrich Wilhelm III. of Prussia died in 1861, and was succeeded by his brother Wilhelm I., whose prime minister was Otto von Bismarck, an exceedingly able man, and one who had no feeling against war, but said that "blood and iron" was the only cure for all the difficulties of Germany. His first war was about the German duchies of Holstein and Lauenburg, which had belonged to the Kings of Denmark just as Hanover did to the Kings of England, and on the death of the last of the male line of Denmark, the Germans declared that they ought not to pass to the new King Christian IX., who inherited in the female line. The Danes on the other hand said that these two duchies were one with Schleswig, and could not be divided, and there was a sharp war, all the Germans, Austrians and all, joining in it. Prussia was much too strong for Denmark, and no one would help the poor little kingdom, and the King was obliged to give up to Prussia and Austria all the three duchies of Schleswig, Holstein and Lauenburg, though the Danes were burning with anger and grief. Then came a dispute between Prussia and Austria, and Wilhelm made an alliance with Victor Emanuel, and promised to go on fighting in Germany until Austria should be forced to give up Venice.

Next Count Bismarck proposed that Prussia should have the North German states, and Austria the South, and that there should be an Assembly elected by all the people to settle the affairs of the Fatherland, as all Germans love to call their country. This came to nothing, and the two great Powers prepared for a great fight as to which should be the real head of Germany. Saxony, Hanover, Hesse-Cassel, and Nassau, though northern states, all took the side of Austria, and sent their forces to join the Austrian army in Bohemia.

Count von Moltke was placed at the head of the Prussian army, and at once sent a division to seize Hesse-Cassel and the Elector in it. Other troops were sent to seize Saxony and Hanover. George V. of Hanover was blind, but he was with his army at Göttingen, trying to join the Bavarians, and his troops gained a victory at Langensalza, but it only served to make the fall of Hanover glorious, and he yielded in June, 1866. Then the Prussians marched into Saxony, and, having mastered that country, entered Bohemia. They were the best armed and best trained soldiers in Germany, and their needle-guns carried all before them. The battle of Koniggrätz, on the 2nd of July, was very hotly contested, and was for a long time doubtful, but in the end the Austrians were forced to retreat, having lost double as many men as the Prussians. Victory after victory followed, and then peace was made at Prague, in August, by which Austria gave up her claims to be a part of Germany, and to have any share in the Confederation.

Moreover, Prussia kept as her own, Hanover, Hesse-Cassel, Nassau, and Frankfurt; and though Bavaria, Saxony, Wurtemburg, and Baden still remained as states, with their own princes over them, they are under the power of Prussia, with an obligation to fight under her in time of war. All the states in the north owned Prussia as their head, and though there was violence and injustice in the means by which the union was brought about, it is good for the people not to have so large a number of very small courts, each with all the expenses of a separate government, and some really depending on the duties on hired horses, and, what was worse, on licences to gaming houses, to which the vicious of all Europe thronged. It is an immense benefit that those at Spa, Baden, and other places were put an end to.

CHAPTER L.

WILHELM I.............. 1870–1877.

THE growth of Prussia, which had only been a kingdom since the seventeenth century, made the French nation jealous and all Europe uneasy.

In the meantime there had been a long course of disturbances in Spain, and the people having driven out their own queen, were looking for a new royal family. They offered their crown to Leopold, Prince of Hohenzollern, a cousin of the King of Prussia; but as soon as the French heard of the plan, they were furious. To prevent war, Leopold at once gave up all intention of being King of Spain; but this would not satisfy the French, who really only wanted an excuse for measuring their strength with that of Prussia, and of trying once more to get the Rhine for their frontier. So the

French ambassador to Prussia met King Wilhelm in the public promenade at Ems, and demanded of him a pledge that under no possible circumstances should Leopold of Hohenzollern ever accept the crown of Spain. Wilhelm did not choose to answer a request so made in such a place. The French declared that he had insulted their ambassador, and war was at once declared. All Germany felt that the real cause of the war was the desire of France to win the lands up to the Rhine; so not only the Prussians, but the newly overcome countries, also the Bavarians and South Germans, felt the matter concerned the Fatherland, and took up arms.

From one end to the other of Germany was sung the song of "the Watch on the Rhine," and the young men went forth to join the army, with the tears and farewells of their families, in a high spirit of devoting themselves for their country. The fight began on the borders of France, Count Moltke being again the manager of the army, though the King was at its head. The French had actually crossed the frontier, under their Emperor himself, boasting and triumphing, and talking of again setting up their eagles at Berlin, and making a great triumph of their first little success. But that was all; at Weissenburg and at Worth they were routed, and again at Saarbrucken, and the Crown Prince of Prussia marched across the Vosges mountains, leaving part of the army to besiege Strasburg. All round Metz, the city where there had been so much warfare between France and Germany, there was fierce fighting, but always the Germans gained, until they had shut one great French army into Metz. Marshal McMahon hastened to help his countrymen, but the Germans met him in the vicinity of Sedan, on the 1st of September, and in another long and terrible battle King William gained the victory. MacMahon was severely wounded, and Napoleon III. was forced to give himself up as a prisoner.

Then the Crown Prince marched on to lay siege to Paris, while his father entered Rheims. The Government which the French had set up declared that they would not part with a foot of ground, and on the other hand the Prussians were resolved that Elsass and Lorraine should be given back to Germany, and so the war went on. The rule the Germans observed was that no person who did not fight should be injured, and that of course real soldiers should be treated as prisoners of war; but if the people of the country shot at them, that they must be treated as robbers and murderers; and if a German were attacked in a village, it was burnt, and one or more of the men put to death. On the whole, these rules were observed; and though there were miseries and horrors, they were not so bad as in former wars.

Strasburg was taken first, then Metz, and the armies which were raised by the French to relieve Paris were beaten before they could come up. All Germany was full of enthusiasm and delight. The South Germans wished to be one again with the North Germans, and King Ludwig II. of Bavaria proposed to the other princes that they should choose the King of Prussia to be German Emperor. Wilhelm was before Paris at the time, living in Versailles, the most splendid palace in France, and there it was that the deputation came to him and offered him the crown of the Empire, and he was proclaimed in the hall of mirrors, so that the old times of proclaiming an Emperor at the head of a victorious army seemed to have come back.

The next day the Parisians tried to sally out, but in vain, and they were nearly starved out, so that they made up their minds to surrender. On the 1st of March a small portion of the troops entered the city, but the feelings of the French were spared by the Emperor, who abstained from making a triumphal entry. A treaty was made by which France had to pay 5,000,000,000 of francs towards

WILHELM 1.

the expenses of the war, and to give up Elsass and Lorraine to Germany. These places had indeed been unjustly gained, but they had belonged to the French for so many years that the inhabitants much disliked the change, and at Strasburg the French tricolor continued for more than a year to wave on the top of the spire of the cathedral, because no one who could climb it safely would go up to put the German eagle in its stead.

The first diet of the Empire was held in 1871, and the constitution was settled; but it is not the same with the old Holy Roman Empire, either in power or size. It only extends over the German soil, and has nothing to do with Italy; and the powers of each of the kingdoms, and other states that belonged to it, are clearly defined. The present Emperor is Wilhelm, son to the Friedrich Wilhelm III. and Louise, who suffered so much from Napoleon I.; and his eldest son, the Crown Prince of Prussia, is married to the eldest daughter of Queen Victoria.

www.ingramcontent.com/pod-product-compliance
Lightning Source LLC
Chambersburg PA
CBHW022058300426
44117CB00007B/507